DRAGONPROOF ECOMMERCE

Visit

www.dragonproofbook.com

for the latest content, strategy, and community resources for your business - absolutely free and utterly essential.

DRAGONPROOF ECOMMERCE

You Vs. Amazon - How To Protect Your Online Business, Products, And Customers

RICK WILSON

The content provided herein is simply for educational purposes and does not take the place of professional advice from your financial advisor. Every effort has been made to ensure that the content provided is accurate and helpful for our readers at the time of publishing.

No warranty is made with respect to the accuracy or completeness of the information contained herein, and the author/publisher specifically disclaims any responsibility for any liability, loss, or risk, personal or otherwise, which is incurred as a consequence, directly or indirectly, of the use and application of any of the contents of this book.

Dragonproof Ecommerce by Rick Wilson, published independently.

ISBN: 9781795220101

Edited by Christopher Barrish

Cover design and illustration by Jenae Loofbourrow

What does it mean to be “dragonproof”?

This is a concept that goes beyond the realm of business, and can apply to all aspects of life. Personal, professional, or spiritual, whatever path you're on, there will always be "dragons" out there. Facing them requires courage. But your fearlessness in these challenges is inexorably linked with a life of personal growth, success, and ultimately, joy. For everyone who is ready to take on their greatest fears, and reach for their biggest dreams, every day in every little way, this book is for you.

ACKNOWLEDGMENTS

Writing a book is not that different from launching a company... for every hour spent alone at a desk, facing that big and seemingly insurmountable task, there is another hour spent drawing upon the wisdom, counsel, encouragement, and energy of those around you. One fuels the other - tireless inner drive, and harmony with the people you create your projects with and for. Our true teachers are the people we see and work with every day, and I am humbled and grateful to the countless inspirational voices that have supported me in my own journey. If I accomplish one thing with this book, it will be to pass on that note of support, encouragement, and inspiration to every single person who opens it.

So, humor me for a moment while I give thanks to some of my teachers - without them this book - and this career, this life, would not have been possible.

First I would like to thank my dear friend, business partner, mentor, and inspiration Russ Carroll. Russ' utterly unique genius encompasses technology, art, and business, and champions the magical places where all three intersect. He is a true pioneer in this great human experience, and I am forever grateful for his guidance and vision.

Thank you to my early employer, the iconic and inspirational author/speaker/coach Brian Buffini - for teaching me that business and sales are not about tricking, coercing, convincing, or cajoling. It's not about stealing a victory or meeting a quota. Great business is a conversation, which should only lead to one place: a better and happier life for ALL parties. This core message of Brian's work has been a guiding principle for me throughout my professional life.

Every day when I come to work, I am surrounded by the most incredibly talented, dedicated, passionate, and hard-working team imaginable - our Miva family. We have a quote on our website describing the sentiment upon which the company was founded and still operates - "anything is possible." I see our ace customer support team, our unparalleled creative professional services department, sharp-as-a-tack managers, unstoppable developers, ingenious designers, spectacular human resource team, sales wizards, marketing and content maestros, 5-star client account reps, brilliant administrative staff, and insanely talented executives tackle projects big and small with ingenuity and zest. I am deeply proud to join them and learn from them, sharing in the enormous trust and good will we have earned with one another and our business' clients.

And to those clients I must also give my deepest and most heartfelt thanks. Our customers, who range from intrepid entrepreneurs starting a home business, to multi-national enterprises earning hundreds of millions of dollars in revenue every year, are a true cross-section of the dream of ecommerce realized. Not just the dream, but the practical reality - the day-to-day, nitty-gritty of running an online business. With evolving economic, cultural, and technological conditions changing under our feet pretty much daily, this is no small accomplishment. Thank you to every business - and by that I mean to every person making those businesses happen - for sharing your dreams with us, and allowing us the great privilege of helping you realize those dreams. It is my sincere hope that this book will encourage you to feel great about all that you have already accomplished, and all that you will soon achieve.

Finally and most importantly, I want to thank my friends and family (and my dogs!) for their unwavering support throughout this process. Thank you for showing up when I needed you, thank you for sharing in my enthusiasm and nurturing it at every turn. From San Diego to San Francisco, from Burning Man to the boardroom, in quiet times and loud times, happy times and tough times, I have been very lucky to be so surrounded with love.

RW

CONTENTS

INTRODUCTION	On Dragons and Hope	xiii
PART I	**Product**	**1**
ONE	Beyond Commodities	5
TWO	Sustainable Margins	17
THREE	A New Approach to Branding Products	25
PART II	**Platform**	**37**
FOUR	Complete Ecommerce	41
FIVE	Integrations Matter	54
SIX	Trust Systems	64
PART III	**Channel**	**79**
SEVEN	One Business, Many Channels	82
EIGHT	Learning From Marketplaces	92
NINE	Scale and Transitions	98
PART IV	**Customer**	**111**
TEN	Personas & Pain Points	115
ELEVEN	Total Personalization	125
TWELVE	Ethical Marketing & Human Data	135
PART V	**Results**	**153**
THIRTEEN	Metrics of Success	157
FOURTEEN	The Future of Ecommerce	164
FIFTEEN	Leadership Qualities	177
CONCLUSION	Bullish on the Future	185
INDEX		188

INTRODUCTION

ON DRAGONS AND HOPE

Will independent ecommerce survive the age of Amazon? Do the tools exist today to protect and support businesses in the face of an aggressive, cunning, trillion-dollar global behemoth which often feels less like an online department store, and more like a dragon circling overhead? This is the question that keeps me up at night. And I'm not alone.

There is a kind of hysteria in the broader ecommerce conversation these days. As CEO of Miva, Inc., creator of the Miva ecommerce platform, I have a front row seat for the real-world concerns of online sellers at every point along the spectrum. In fact, I have a view from the stage.

Every year, our company hosts a gathering for customers, developers, designers, and service providers, to discuss industry trends, explore new features, and network with our peers. On the first morning of the event, the lights dim, the music surges, and I step onto the stage to rally the crowd. Let's get into it! What's the state of our business? What's the health of our community? What tools should we use... which voices should we trust? The mood is magical, optimistic. And then in the audience, that hand goes up... One person, and then another, and then another, have questions about "the Amazon situation." It's like the collective id of the entire industry raising its hand, with mounting urgency.

Is "the everything store" as we know it today the beginning or the end? Should I sell my products to Amazon and let them set the price? Are

Marketplace fees worth the death blow they deal to my margins? Can I manage a complicated multi-tier strategy procuring, marketing, selling, and distributing my products from and to a variety of different "home bases," and still be able to reach the people I want to reach, earn a profitable living, support the infrastructure of my business as it scales, keep the livelihood of my workers strong and safe? Is Amazon's current model, and market share, the status quo for time to come, or will the rules be changed and the rug pulled out from me next week?

Increasingly, concerns over how to deal with the ever-growing "threat" of marketplaces are dominating the discourse - concerns which, if left unaddressed, threaten to harden into outright panic. With Amazon claiming a full 50% of all online sales as of 2019, this is more than just a hot topic, it is a question of raw survival. So the hysteria just might be justified.

That's not much help when you're standing under a spotlight facing the real concerns of real businesspeople whose livelihoods are on the line. We all need answers, practical solutions rooted in honesty and truth.

I don't think we're talking about "tips and tricks" or short-term workflow hacks. There are endless miles of web content articles explaining how to reduce abandoned carts, or out-game the SEO overlords, how to enroll in FBA. Best practices are essential to understand, but I think this moment goes far deeper - it's a story about independence and control. "How, as a seller, do I deal with Amazon?" is really a saga about the advancing digitization of the human experience, which touches so many other aspects of how we live and what we care about right now. In a sense, the Amazon platform is another kind of "stage" upon which we are daily determining what it means to grow, sustainably, as a society. The stakes couldn't be higher.

So yes, your fears are justified. Yes, there is a "dragon" scorching the earth. No, no single one of us will be able to take it down, erase its influence, beat its Q4. But... I believe there is a way forward. Just as in a forest fire, some animals can smell the warning signs well in advance, and many move to safety long before the smoke reaches them. Then when the flames die, a newly-cleared land becomes the basis for new growth, new life. "Dragonfire" is no different.

I am writing this book because I want to empower my peers with the tools - and the armor - to thrive, no matter what the season, no matter what the skies bring. When to plant, when to hide, when to step outside and stand fearlessly in the sun. Together, we are going to explore what's possible, what's at risk, and hopefully arrive at *new foundational perspectives* to help us navigate the growing pains of our time.

The greatest opportunities come when conditions look the bleakest. Frankly, this has been a hard-earned viewpoint that has arisen for me over many years, projects, successes, and stumbles. Ecommerce has been on a similar journey, snatching victory from the jaws of defeat over and over, finally landing in a place of confidence and wisdom that seems inevitable now, but which naysayers predicted would never come. It's been quite a ride.

When I began my professional career, bursting out of business school eager to conquer the markets and rule the world, I ran up against a significant problem: staking out a living in the financial sector was difficult. Joyless. Wits and good intentions were rarely a match for the large institutional sharks which seemed to prey upon the masses and crowd out the upstarts. Around the same time, American retailers were facing a similar problem. Several decades of Walmart's soft monopoly had combined with the residual effects of other mega-retailers' colonization of the American buying experience, to create a toxic stagnation, felt most by the consumer.

It was this moment, right here, that I learned a key lesson which would inform my total worldview, and be the genesis of a new movement in my own life, just as surely as it was on a macro-scale for the industry I would soon enter. **When the old solutions no longer work, we must apply technology to solve it better.** As simple as that.

I looked at how the existing solution was no longer working for people. I thought about the pain which the everyday enterprise felt: How does a business exist? What drives people to come to work in the morning? How does it all thrive or fail – this was, and is, my interest. In my case, the new "technology" was retraining myself as a self-development speaker, sales manager, and then as an architect in the developing world of ecommerce.

The pain which retailers and shoppers had been feeling through the 90s cried out for a better solution. Bloated malls were an inefficient slog, retail was lethargic. It was hard for consumers to find what they needed when they needed it, and it was hard for sellers to connect with those consumers. And so collectively, we applied this new technology called the internet to make the shopping experience better, more profitable, and more effective for everybody. That was the dream of ecommerce, and it only came about in a time of crisis. It came about *because* of the crisis.

Once you accept that basic principle, that *crisis begets better solutions*, doesn't it take the sting out of whatever today's battles and hardships are? I think so. And with this in mind, we'll take on the dragons. We'll look for ways to change our perspective on the dragon *du jour*, Amazon, and even find joy in the challenge. Yes, there is joy in the fight! Call it "disruption" if you like, or simply think of it as an exhilarating mountain to climb. I do.

This is the kind of thinking I reach for when I look out at the audience and see that sea of hands raised, each one unsure if independence and prosperity can endure while a dragon is breathing fire upon the land. Well, as with all creative endeavors, we don't have all the answers at the start. Where would the fun be in that?

Thank you for joining me on this journey. I am confident that we will both leave this experience armed with new knowledge, new strategies, and most importantly, new *hope*. Let's take a good look at our assumptions and turn them on their ear. Let's recalibrate our *thinking* first, and let that be the guide for recalibrating our *action*. And above all, let's enjoy the ride!

PART I: PRODUCT

What are you selling?

This is the natural first question that I ask new clients. It's also the first question that a consumer asks of a business. But the answer is not as straightforward as it seems. Does a bike shop sell bicycles? Or do they sell "transportation"? Do they sell physical fitness? Do they sell fashion? Do they sell a faster way to get to work than walking? Do they sell convenience? Do they, in a sense, sell time? Of course the answer is they sell all of these things. If this business is building a working strategy for what to order, how to sell, where to sell, and who to sell to, they must learn to look at a bike as more than a bike. It is aluminum and rubber housing a very specific set of solutions - answers to problems which drive people to buy. Answers which bring relief. Answers which justify a business' reason for existing, give its products value, and ultimately protect it against all contenders.

The first bike I ever wanted to own was a Redline. To a 10-year-old kid, this bike was the *premiere* BMX experience. Gleaming chrome tubular forks, that v-shaped handlebar, "rugged" styling (according to the edgy taste of a pre-teen), in magnificently 80s colors like "Radberry"...I just *had* to have it. Now this was well before the days of big box stores selling these kind of bikes. You went to the neighborhood shop with your mom and picked all the parts you wanted right off the wall. Looking back, this was not that dissimilar from today's modern ecommerce experience. To a wide-eyed kid making every choice live in the showroom, this was an incredible buying experience! Total choice x instant gratification. And, at 10, I'm issuing commands to the salesperson like a pro, "I want that color, but those handlebars, and this seat..." etc., and I'm literally building this machine on the spot, one that could accommodate my exact needs - a frame long enough to support my early growth spurt, a coaster brake on the pedals because I didn't know how to operate handlebar brakes, and a color which matched the style of the other kids' bikes on my block.

I think it will be helpful to all of us if we start looking at our "bicycles" as answers. The 10-year old boy got this. Look, you can easily learn how to assign attributes on a product page. The thing that can't be explained in a 3-line bullet list is how to challenge, decimate, revise, and improve your perception of how and why you do the things you do. This is the gold.

At the major inflection points of my own life, success or failure has always hinged upon my ability to reinvent my own perception of evolving conditions - so much more so than raw technical expertise, or even good luck, though you need those too. So my hope here is that we can look at ways to adapt and evolve our *perception* of the day's conditions, through the specific prism of ecommerce principles and techniques.

This is the direction of the book you are about to read - it's not a technical manual, and it's not "Amazon for dummies" - let's be honest, that type of content would be utterly outdated in 5 or 6 months anyway. Rather, let's look at fundamental approaches which will ***protect*** your products, through every technological leap and every cultural shift. Let's hack our own perceptions of how our businesses work. This foundational approach will have a timeless quality - meaning, it will still serve you when best practices, trends, and technologies move and evolve in the short term - and they will.

A content writer came to me the other day with a list of tweets featuring the hashtag #slaythebeast, as part of a campaign for featuring ecommerce products in ways which might "beat" competition with similar items hosted on Amazon. But is this mentality really serving us? The 20-year rise of Amazon as a cultural institution, economic monopoly, and "gatekeeper" of ecommerce is clearly a massive paradigm shift which poses an existential threat to all businesses. However, we must not tackle this moment by trying to "slay the beast" - honestly that fight is far too stacked to win. But by reimagining and fortifying our own role, our own importance, our own power - through our products - we find the path forward.

These ideas will be communicated to your customers, and will guide *their* understanding of what it is exactly that you sell, and why.

CHAPTER ONE

BEYOND COMMODITIES

500 MILLION SOLUTIONS

At the time of this writing, there are as many as 25 million ecommerce stores online. And then there is Amazon. With 50% market share of all online retail purchases in the bag by this decade's end, and a full 15% of all sales, anywhere, online or off, Amazon's intimidating dominance cannot be ignored. There are nearly 500 million products hosted there. Of this staggering figure, it is highly likely that whatever type of item you are selling will be in some way represented there by other sellers. And if not, if you've got the magical whatsit that no other brand has thought of, it's a good bet that Amazon will poach it, either by cornering you into selling it at their price and on their terms, or by simply knocking it off completely and taking away the keys to your third party independence altogether. So what separates the products on your shelf from 500,000,000 other options - why must it exist?

The question itself would have been unimaginable just a few years ago. But consumers have adapted very quickly to *choice on an unfathomable scale*. Really, the concept of a forever-increasing product selection was always the core of retail's march through the 20th century. We see it right from the start. In a real sense, ecommerce began with the primitive (by today's standards) mail order distribution business pioneered by Sears at the dawn of the 1900s. Whereas a rural shopper had previously only known the goods at a local mom & pop, suddenly the Sears Catalog gave them easy access to hundreds of pages of alternatives, shipped right to their door. This sounds familiar. In order to survive that moment, the original retailers had to find ways to highlight the unique value of *their* goods against the world's, and so too must today's sellers. It's just that the playing field now is *so* much vaster.

Then as now, **the product is the center of all ecommerce.** Everything else that surrounds it - shopping experience, brand, fulfilment, community - are all secondary. So to even begin to attack this question of how to remain viable in the face of a massive marketplace of alternatives, I think it's valuable to look at our products in a new light.

The interesting thing about products is that they are better expressed by what they *do* rather than what they *are*.

Through my work with Miva, I have encountered every conceivable type of product. If you can imagine it, someone is selling it, from motor oil to mobile cranes, hand-drawn illustrations to complex software systems. Most sellers are able to eloquently describe what their product *is*. It is powered by USB. It costs $10. It comes in green.

Oftentimes, trends and innovations which sweep the mainstream shopping world get their start on small ecommerce sites years before items get popular on a grander scale. I've seen everything from gluten-free dog treats, to orthotic mattresses shipped in a box, to international matchmakers, years before holistic pet food, digital mattress builds, and Tinder became hot markets. I think the reason for this is that smaller ecommerce sellers are operating at such small scale that they have more leeway to bet the farm on a hunch, and more ability to fulfill small-scale experiments. Larger sellers can glean the surviving ideas from the top of the pile, and copy at enormous scale.

In this way, ecommerce is the medium through which products are born and ultimately "communicated" to the world. The ideas spread not just through ecommerce, but *because* of ecommerce.

However, when you are up against that wall of 500 million competitors, the conversation must reach deeper than just attributes and categories. Before we can even begin to develop an Amazon strategy, we have to come into an understanding of an individual product's unique deserving of attention. There must be a reason for its existence, a reason to buy it at all, a reason to buy it *from you.*

This is the heart of *non-commodification.* Why is this version of this product relevant to me, the potential buyer? In order to assess this, we must immediately ask, what does the product *solve* for? Does it makes some task I have to perform easier? Does it bring sustenance, joy, knowledge, entertainment? Does it fulfill a need or desire? Does it at least *offer* to do these things, regardless of whether or not it succeeds? These are all "do"-oriented ways of looking at a product.

Is a "product" another way of saying "a solution" for the customer? Ooh that's good. Right off the bat, by looking at a product as the very thing that eases a consumer's specific pain point, we imbue our product, and our business, with *a reason for existing.* Solution-consciousness forms the true basis for value.

What the product *is* is less important than what it *solves* for.

Here is a fundamental truth which feels obvious once you say it, but which is not adequately expressed for the vast majority of products. I have set it apart from the text above because I believe it's important - as we move through more fundamental perspective shifts, I will continue to present more ideas like this in the same format. These basic tenets of doing business, specifically online, have been arrived at through closely observing how some ecommerce sellers get it right, and some miss the mark.

One of the more heartbreaking phenomena in ecommerce is when a seller is sitting on a very unique, very solution-oriented product, and they don't realize it or capitalize on it. They get stuck in that "is," and fail to make a compelling case for "do." This happens often, but we don't hear about it so much for a simple reason - the products in question get lost in the shuffle and the companies go under. Getting your head around the unique *solutions* of your products is job one - this simple shift in how you're defining them can create *huge* results.

An apparel manufacturer I've worked with for many years, SCOTTeVEST, first walked in the door with an amazingly unique product. They basically reinvented the shape, placement, and function of something so common it's on almost every garment you own - the pocket. SCOTTeVEST figured out that different activities, jobs, sports, etc. all required wildly specific and different utility from clothing. They looked at the way people lived and worked, and realized that "everyday carry" tools, devices, and gear came in many sizes and virtually no modern clothing prepared for this. So they created it. Only problem was, they didn't initially seize on this "unique solution to help you carry your stuff" angle as the main messaging for the brand, and instead focused on price. Deep discount sales would move the needle temporarily, but discounting wasn't enough of a hook to re-convert customers again and again. So, SCOTTeVEST shifted gears, changing all messaging to indicate what was *different* about products from mass-market retail garments, by expressing what the clothing could *do*. Our job as ecommerce platform designers was to support this message by creatively showing what the product *solved*, right on the home page. Now this was a great basis for enduring customer relationships. *Here is apparel that helps me have an easier day*. With this approach, the business grew dramatically.

Too many sellers do not elaborate on the "do" of their wares and stay stuck in the "is." The result is just noise for a consumer. Endless choices, which all vaguely feel like the same thing. This is a problem we want to fight.

Right away, we want to frame the entire story of a business in terms of what it can *do* for its customers, via its products. **To the extent that a business can use technology to produce, distribute, and market that product to the audience which needs the solution it provides, the more value that product has.** We've just summed up the core principle of this entire book, and all commerce, really. This is a message we will return to again and again as we dive deeper into the story of how products - your products - can connect with the people who need and want them. ***Products are solutions.***

Trick question: What is the difference between solving for the customer's pain vs. solving for your business' pain? Are they one and the same? No. A customer who needs a faster bike obviously has a different pain point than a bicycle manufacturer who needs to produce and sell those bikes faster. But these two goals harmonize around the same point - *the product as a vessel for solving problems.* It doesn't matter if it's red or blue. *How does it solve my problem?* That's the definition of a product, and it's a major key to protecting it.

The greater specificity with which you can define your *solution*, the less like all the other similar widgets on Amazon's shelf it will appear.

COMMODITY VS. PRODUCT

Most people have a casual understanding of commodities from investment markets. We generally think of commodities as global *staples* like oil, corn, coffee, sugar - anything that is widely used as a "raw" component of other manufacturing, or anything that is farmed directly from the earth. The key attribute which defines commodities in an ecommerce context is interchangeability - lack of specialness, in a sense, lack of difference. In this way, "headphones" are a commodity, while Bose Soundsport Wireless Earbuds are a specialized product. The difference is in *the specificity of the solution.* Headphones solve for customers' need to listen to audio from a personal device. Commodity. Bose Wireless Earbuds solve for customers' need to listen to audio via small wearable Bluetooth in-ear modules, while performing activities which make wires cumbersome, and which deliver high quality audio consistent with other products produced by the Bose brand. Non-commodity. There are at least 50,000 pairs of headphones listed on Amazon. There is one pair of Bose Soundsports.

Non-commodified ecommerce is about more than just brand name, though. Commodities are roughly interchangeable with comparable items from any producer. Non-commodities are uniquely *customized* by manufacturer, with distinctive utility, quality, or aesthetics. Commodities are mass-produced and easily acquired. Non-commodities' supply is *limited* by the total output of a given individual manufacturer. Commodities' value is determined by the class of goods, rather than the individual good. Non-commodities' value reflects a *unique relationship* between this vendor, this item, and this customer.

Unfortunately, you may not be the only person in the history of the cosmos to offer your type of product. But can you find a way to explain why the way *you* make it, or the way *you* offer it, is unlike the others? Can you focus that explanation around a solution-oriented "do"?

Quick anecdote: when I was a school-age kid, I had very curly hair. I was the only one in my class with curls, and as you might suspect, I was teased mercilessly for it. "Difference" is not a celebrated quality for third graders. But something wonderful happened when I was an adult - I realized that this difference was not a drawback, but a *positive* attribute. It's fun and unique, and I have embraced how having a look that is slightly different from the crowd makes me stand out in a *good* way.

If you are selling an interchangeable commodity, there is *technically* **no reason for your business to exist.** This is why, these days, we love the idea of "curly hair."

Non-commodity does not necessarily mean "so niche that only one person in America needs to buy it." But in a larger sense, if there are more than 1000 ear thermometers on Amazon (there are), I, as a consumer, need to know what your ear thermometer solves for that the others don't. That's the essence of non-commodification. It's ~~a~~ *the* critical piece of leverage you will need to understand and express about every item you sell. Not simply as a marketing ploy, but as an essential *raison d'être* for your entire project.

What makes *my* product discrete, necessary, and valuable? On a deeper level, it's like asking, *"how can I celebrate my difference?"*

Most of us, as we grow up, feel insecure about a variety of things, but then hopefully, as we earn wisdom, find a sense of peace and security with who we really are. With the hair, I finally got to a point of not wanting to stress out about trying to make myself into something else. It was the beginning of a "pulling on a string" that led to me finding more confidence, and freeing up more headspace to address other topics.

I think we see the same thing with ecommerce businesses, especially towards the beginning of their organization. There is a strong push-pull between trying to fit in (commodify) and trying to stand out (non-commodify). It all plays out in the products.

DETERMINING VALUE

Do you like soy milk? Personally, I can't stand the gritty taste of it in my coffee, but I have a good friend who is allergic to cow's milk and has subsequently become obsessed with finding the world's greatest soy half-and-half.

This distinction to me expresses how *common products elicit totally different experiences*. Same bean, same milk, but for my friend it provides a solution, while for me it stands in the way of a solution. In this same way, you might say that *a product's value is completely variable based upon the way it intersects with a unique problem*.

The natural unfolding of this idea is right there on the shelf: soy milk, almond milk, cashew milk, hemp milk, rice milk, coconut milk, and other non-dairy milks are currently selling more than 2 billion dollars worth of product every year. I don't see this so much as "competition" with dairy milk, but as increasingly dialed-in solutions for increasingly specific customer needs.

A product's value is determined by the strength, or lack thereof, of the solution which defines it.

What gives a product value in a crowded marketplace? Especially if there are 1 or 100 or 1000 other versions of the same thing out there? It must offer **solutions relevant to specific customer problems**. We assess value by looking through *their* eyes. One man's nourishment is another man's bad flavor. When thinking about the value of a particular product, there are many factors which can connote value, but *only* relative to a particular problem being solved.

This will be very helpful to you when choosing products to sell, and then describing them to your customers. Offer benefits. Fix problems. Be a helpful component. Soy milk is a great alternative for people who are allergic to cow milk - that's a strong, valuable solution. Its color, consistency, and even taste are not as relevant/valuable to an audience of customers with dairy allergies - they just need milk which won't cause a reaction. And if you have identified this audience at the outset of building your business, soy milk will be a great product to sell.

These ideas are obviously not limited to selling online, but they are essential to selling online. **Products are answers, and value is the strength of solutions relative to a specific problem or viewpoint.** This should always be the basis for what you sell.

A GUIDE TO CHOOSING THE RIGHT PRODUCTS - FROM THE HEART

Phil Knight ran track in college. Steve Jobs grew up in a California neighborhood of electronic engineers. Richard Branson sold records through the mail as a teenager. The products these larger-than-life entrepreneurs would later create for Nike, Apple, and Virgin were, in a very real sense, solutions to problems they directly knew and experienced from a young age. Make high quality running shoes more affordable for more people. Bring the power of sophisticated computing into every home. Distribute music from all over the world to people around the world. By applying innovative technology and business practices to existing consumer desire, these companies, and many others like them, transcended the shifting conditions of the eras they were born in to endure and thrive across generations.

Wouldn't it be wonderful to apply some of that same juju to the business you are running/working for/dreaming up right now? **The path-**

way to competitive, enduring products is less paved with market research and more driven by emotion, heart, experience, and instinct. This is where the real winners are born. Of the many ecommerce projects I've had the pleasure of working on with Miva, the ones that have found the most success have been those which applied life passion to problem-solving, applied real world experience and human intuition to improve the lives of real-world people.

> ***Practical* solutions are rooted in *emotional* inspiration - how we feel about the skills, resources, and experience we have already achieved.**

That's actually really nice advice to give to someone who's in business - from a personal standpoint, reach towards finding a sense of peace and security in what you *already* are and what you *already* do. Problems you have encountered and the solutions which have worked for you. Celebrating what's already *unique*, as opposed to following a pack and trying to fit in.

If, as a business, I'm just trying to force myself into this box of commodified things that I see in the world, it's almost impossible to discover new products to sell or new shopping experiences to offer. Fitting in is not a virtue here, and so we have to seize upon whatever unique assets and attributes we already possess.

It is certain that there are resources you already have as a potential entrepreneur which could be serving you. Don't sit there thinking, "well, what would Apple do? Or what would Google do?" (Because you're not Apple or Google.) Instead ask, "what are the tools I have at my disposal? Is there anything I can do with them that would be unique and different that would bring me closer to the solutions that *I* personally seek?" Then use those answers to look for a business idea.

Sometimes one or more of the people you work with is this unique element, and can be the source of future product ideas, in the way you choose to apply their talents to you project. It's incredibly powerful to build a business around a person who's got a great skill, if there is a human already on your team who is the unique and amazing asset in your arsenal. In your case it might be a product designer you already employ, or perhaps a competitive advantage like a pre-existing personal relationship with an importer. In Miva's case, we began our unique journey with a brilliant and talented software developer named Jon Burchmore. John has an incredible skill at scalable database architectures, which we determined we could apply to ecommerce in a novel way. So, building a business around someone like Jon is smart, because he's a great resource that you're applying uniquely, versus just waking up one day and deciding, "I want to go build a new widget because I see others like it are popular, but I don't know anything about that industry. Let me see if I can go hire someone I've never met."

How will you apply technology - any kind of technology - to address the pain points in customers' lives in a new and different way than anyone has before? What's the intersection of your natural interest with those pre-existing problems? What exclusive quality of your wares is no one else offering? What is your current ability to reach the people who stand to buy your product, and how will you interact with them to deliver solutions? How will you creatively express the value of your product as a testament to the strength of those solutions? Answer these questions, and you'll have your product roster, even if right now it's just aspirational. Furthermore, you'll be *protecting* them, because you are inherent to what defines them. Irreplaceable you.

This is the only plausible path to creating, developing, nurturing, and selling products which can hold their own against that wall of 500,000,000 rivals.

DE-COMMODIFYING A COMMODITY PRODUCT

How can a distributor of products which might be considered commodities approach carving out a relevant, competitive place for their business? Customers who don't know your brand, launching a search for "ground coffee" or "flatscreens," etc., will be looking at *pages* of commodified, totally interchangeable options. So how does this kind of seller stand out?

Another Miva client, Plant Therapy, offers a strikingly clear example of transforming what could be a commodity product into an irreplaceable non-commodity. As sellers of essential oils, Plant Therapy excels at adding a *story* and a *personality* to what might otherwise be a very common product category. Yes, a shopper can find lavender oil at any health food market. So why should they buy Plant Therapy's lavender oil? That's where the story comes in.

For this brand, storytelling comes in the form of an overall personalized buying process which knows to pair cardamom with geranium, shares customer feedback about how to use Tea Tree oil to cure common skin conditions, and offers subscriptions for the ease of repeat purchasing. All of the "other stuff" around the product becomes incredibly important in positioning this brand's merchandise as especially oriented to solving unique problems. Everything from unique shopping experience, unique community experience, and great marketing play a role. Plant Therapy combines all of those things to create an assured, "expert" environment around its goods. Simply browsing the site is educational and inspiring to anyone interested in the topic, and this confident wealth of knowledge creates a solution-oriented context of value around every suggestion the site makes to consumers.

The product is still the product, in this case it literally is a commodity, but all of the elements which Plant Therapy surround it with elevate that bottle of essential oil to a status of being unique in the marketplace. In this way, the shopping experience they build around their oils and the way that they employ marketing actually become *a part of the product*. It's the commodity *plus*. The "plus" is the context vis-à-vis specific use case problems ("I don't know which oils to combine," "I need to heal a skin condition," "Buying essential oil every month can be a hassle," etc.).

We'll explore how to use shopping experience and content to elevate value more in later chapters, but for now, keep thinking about the connection between unique solutions and successful solutions. This thinking is somewhat different from the old saw "Do what you love and the money will follow." Here, we're saying: **Express *why* you see this product as the ultimate solution, and the money will follow.**

DEFINE YOUR SOLUTION

Core Problem	01	State the core issue which this brand exists to solve.
Identify Who	02	Who typically experiences these problems?
Past Solutions	03	Which products & workarounds have those people previously relied upon?
New Solutions	04	What new twist, convenience, or clarity are you offering?
Emotional Goal	05	How might customers feel upon using your products?
Your Expertise	06	What special experience does your brand have to answer specific needs?
Points of Access	07	How easy is it to access your products?
Price	08	Why is your margin earned?
Alignment With Mission	09	How do your products directly support your mission statement?
Brand Slogan	10	How does your slogan directly answer the main customer pain point?

CHAPTER TWO

SUSTAINABLE MARGINS

A MARGIN YOU CAN LIVE WITH

For many businesses, Amazon has turned the concept of a "loss leader" into a self-imposed prison. This potentially unsustainable play can be driven by more of a break-even mentality than ambition. But understanding the interplay between innate product value and the margin we can "get away with" charging for it is essential for the survival of all ecommerce businesses.

Selecting products which you will be able to realistically sell at sustainable margins is obviously central to the health of your business. What I'd like to explore in this chapter is a new way of looking at what margin is really a measure of, how to determine it from that basis, and how to use it to set the stage for your brand's entire m.o.

Price is less relevant than most sellers think. The margin's the thing.

Here's a quick example from the field which illustrates a very common problem for ecommerce sellers, which I'll call for the sake of this discussion "**price addiction**." I once consulted for an apparel distributor who ran a relatively simple online-only import business. This seller purchased t-shirts and hats in quantity from a factory in Hong Kong, added branding to the items, and then sold them on the brand's U.S.-based ecommerce site at a 50% markup. The brand's main sales pitch for its items was price - comparable U.S.-made items were still far more costly. To support this idea, the brand was in nearly *perpetual* discount mode. And when orders were sluggish, prices were routinely slashed dangerously close to actual costs. This technique worked, to a point. "Crazy" discounting has always been an effective marketing device, and the brand would see brief surges in orders in step with the severity of the discount. The rush of increased conversions was irresistible to the seller, prompting more price reductions, and more resources devoted to getting the word out about those reductions. The thinking was that higher volume would compensate for the plummeting margins, but alas this was simply not a sustainable long term strategy. The increased costs to order and import more goods, coupled with increased ad buys, plus more human time required to manage traffic and put out fires, left the seller operating on credit. Meanwhile, the brand's customers had now been trained to expect extreme price slashing at regular intervals, resulting in decimated sales for non-discount items.

The health of your margin is the health of your business. Little sacrifices to make more conversions at the expense of margin have a habit of snowballing. The only good answer to this problem is to select high-value products at the outset, products which will not need to be placed in the bargain basement in order to move units, and then *protect them*. We discussed how to look at real product value as a function of "solution" in the previous chapter. With that in mind, how should sellers think of margin?

I'd like to offer that the distance between cost and price is not "what I can get away with selling it for," nor is it "taking my lumps" in order to max out a conversion ratio. Margin is not the value of a product. **Margin is *your* value.**

Margin = the perceived value which *you* bring to the table, in your role of creating and distributing your product to consumers.

It's great to think of margin as a premium the end consumer pays for your services (as opposed to them having to conceive of, produce, and procure the product themselves). There's nothing "tricky" about this - there's no subterfuge, you're not "getting away with" anything by setting your price. This is about understanding the value of your product's solution, plus the value of your role, which is almost like a second solution. Not only will this product bring relief to the customer's pain point, but the team which sells it is further solving the ability of the customer to easily connect with that product. Each of those two solutions has a financial value.

An interesting aspect of quantifying these solutions in dollars is that there is no objective playbook which lists how much each is worth. It really comes down to *belief*, doesn't it?

How much do you think you're worth?

How much is your time and ingenuity worth? What is the price of your experience? That's the conceptual basis of the markup which you can charge for any product over the actual costs which surround its total life cycle. *Belief goes both ways in this case* - how much you, and the customer, believe these solutions are worth. Lining up these two beliefs - theirs and yours - is a wonderful guideline for pricing.

So, the margin is really **an expression of the agreed-upon value of the *company* selling the product.** That should be helpful. And it's definitely not derived from an algorithm.

We are starting to hear more and more stories about Amazon asking vendors to lower prices on their goods. To be certain, this is the result of analytical analysis performed by a spreadsheet. The spreadsheet doesn't know your customer, doesn't know why they need what they need, and can only adapt to those needs after-the-fact by Monday-morningquarterbacking off of previous sales figures. It's just not the complete picture, and it fails to protect the relationship between product and buyer, between product and its competitors. It's an unsustainable race to the bottom, a race to commodification.

To get back to the "price addicted" example above, that seller based crucial decisions about acceptable margins around an adrenaline-fueled game of cat and mouse with their customer. That's why the model was unsustainable. The same products could easily have sold for a higher price point if the brand's total value prop emphasized the work the brand was putting in as importer/curator/supply chain task manager, as opposed to trying to out-discount itself at every opportunity. The problem here wasn't bad marketing, *it was a lack of self-respect*, respect which was certainly due, as any seller who has wrangled the ins and outs of international importing can surely attest.

Thusly, we again see how the emotional set of the seller comes into play. Whether you are making products by hand or orchestrating their movement from other providers, *what you are doing is worth something*. You'd be surprised how many sellers are not automatically coming from this place. Amazon's price algorithms certainly aren't.

Also, note the use of the word "perceived" in the above perspective. That's big. To be viable, **a margin must reflect value which the consumer mentally and emotionally concludes upon reviewing everything you have to say.** There is nothing "objective" about it.

With this caveat, we are acknowledging that **a "secret" value which a company provides is hardly a value.** The customer must be shown clearly that your version of this product is inherently more valuable than the others, first because of the unique solution it provides, and second *because of what you add to the pot*. We will explore some excellent ways to express these concepts to customers later in this chapter. When selling online in a competitive field, product selection and margin-setting *driven by confident belief* sets you up for success.

Margin is also what the customer agrees it is worth paying for them *not to have to do it*, in a sense. No jewelry customer reasonably considers whether or not to build a mining rig to extract gold deposits from the earth, enroll in a 4-year art school to learn how to weld together a bracelet, and apprentice for a decade with a master craftsman to learn techniques for stone setting. But if it is clear that you have done these things, and that competitors who also sell bracelets lack the visionary skills to produce goods as beautiful as yours, then a customer will gladly pay your markup over whatever your raw materials cost.

That's what they're paying you for. *It's the product plus you.* The more unique in the marketplace / challenging-to-produce / innovative-vs-what's-come-before your product is, relative to what other producers are offering or what a consumer would have to do to make the product themselves, the higher your margin can be. It has very little to do with what other rings are selling for on Amazon this week. You conceive of it, you produce it or procure it, you present it, you distribute it, you build a community around it, and all for the benefit of answering the customer's questions, relieving their pain. What is *that* worth?

MARGINS AND AMAZON

Amazon's fee structure has created an unusual conundrum for all sellers, even those who don't use their services. As Amazon market share increases, so too does the number of Amazon sellers (4 million vendor accounts, growing at a rate of about 1000/day). Every one of those businesses will have to agree to Amazon's fees, and set their own margins accordingly - even as an "independent" third-party vendor on the site. So, for a growing majority of ecommerce vendors, Amazon fees will be "baked in" to the product prices. Is this a defensible position?

The bottom line is this: **if your margins aren't big enough to support Amazon's merchant fees, you probably won't have a viable business long term.** This is not because you have to sell via Amazon - you don't. It's because the emerging realities of margin across *all* channels reflect Amazon's presence. In a sense, Amazon merchants will be setting price standards for their own industries - on the high end (inflated pricing to absorb some of Amazon's fees), and on the low-end (the small margin they will be able to keep after Amazon takes its slice).

How does this dovetail with what we've already observed about the nature of solutions, value, and confidence, with price as their combined manifestation?

Amazon essentially creates its own margin by reducing yours - that's its business model. If you want the services that a marketplace provides you have to pay for them. But if enough other sellers want those services, you have to pay for that too - by adjusting pricing to fit within or undercut the new standards they have now all set for the economy. Amazon subscription fees, referral fees, closing fees and more can easily add up to an additional 50% you'd have to factor into your product price - so, you can either hike up the price which the consumer sees, or keep the price competitive and eat as much of the 50% as possible in order to retain the business. Neither option is appealing, and both seem to negate the foundational concept of a value-driven margin. But unfortunately, out-gaming Amazon's fees via pricing adjustments says, "the value I offer is determined by arbitrary external factors, not by the solutions I am providing for customers." Unsustainable. So how do we marry these diverging realities?

Amazon's fees should be *covered* by your margins, but these fees must not *dictate* the margin.

Many Miva clients that I work with everyday successfully utilize some form of Amazon services to complement an independent ecommerce site, from FBA fulfilment to fully-realized Amazon brand pages. Some employ the Merchant Fulfilled Network to share shipping and order control with Amazon, while others offer Seller Fulfilled Prime to trade on the ubiquity of Prime while still maintaining total control over the handling of inventory. But in every case, I recommend that these clients **set pricing to reflect the true value prop, and then, only choose Amazon services which can be covered by that margin.** Not the other way around. This approach *protects* the value of the product/brand overall.

If you use Amazon as your lowest margin, especially if you're receiving Amazon storage and let's say 40 and 50 percent of the money collected, and can still turn a profit, your ability to continue turning a profit out of your own direct-to-consumer model should be assured.

We land here at a great business practice. If I can figure out how to make ten cents when I sell something for a dollar, and I know I can sell enough of those things that I'm going to survive, I've established a great baseline. Once I get that going, *then* I can start looking for ways to create more efficiency and increase the margin gradually, patiently, wherever I can. How do I make that ten cents into eleven cents, and eleven cents into fifteen?

Who are the businesses that are the most successful at that model? Who has taken that model to the absolute ridiculous extreme? Ikea and Walmart leap to mind. Walmart took the efficiency model where fractions of pennies matter because they sell *so many* things. Ikea may offer an office chair very close to its actual cost and sell a healthy amount of them, but then it off-sets that low margin by encouraging purchase of high-margin impulse buys like $10 kitchen rags before customers get to checkout.

Again, your apples are not Walmart or Ikea's oranges. But these are principles that you can use and learn from. If you can hypothetically sell via Amazon, pay their fees, and sell enough to still make a profit in that process, then it's worth your time to make that profit. Then you can start looking for ways to improve your margin, perhaps by adding more direct sales into the mix.

INCREASING VALUE

There are many practical ways to increase margins - all of them embody the idea of *applying technology to improve solutions*. This doesn't mean that all solutions are software/systems-based, or non-creative. "Improved solutions" encompasses gains in *logistics*, such as more effective supply chain management, *strategy*, such as shortening that supply chain by selling direct to consumer from manufacturing, and *public perception*, like using digital branding to increase reach/desire/exclusivity of goods. All of these are technological solutions to complex problems.

Again, **margin is really an expression of the value add which a seller brings to the product they sell.** So to increase the margin, it follows that you have to increase that (perceived and real) value. This is the perspective shift. *"How can I compete with the Amazon shopping experience/ship speed/social integration/marketing reach, etc."* versus *"How can increase the value add my company is bringing to this already valuable product?"* **The former pits you against a dragon in an unwinnable game of catch-up, the latter orients you to fortifying and nurturing your own operations.**

Here's an example... from 1962. Earlier, I alluded to the idea of the Sears Catalog as a forerunner to modern ecommerce, and it was. By the mid-1900s though, the Sears empire had evolved away from mail order and into an enormous country-wide physical footprint. While the company focused on opening more and more retail stores, overhead and inventory control had gotten away from them - solution-deficits which were passed on to consumers in the form of less effective shopping experiences, less goods on local shelves, and higher prices for those goods.

Enter the Brothers Walton, who built upon a single discount five-and-dime shop in Rogers, Arkansas, with an innovative application of technology. Walmart envisioned the creation of far larger, yet fewer stores, strategically placed close to distribution hubs, which could deliver products to shelves faster and in much greater quantities than conventional retailers. We don't know if Walmart initially set out to "beat" Sears and become a 400-billion-dollar-dragon of its own - but we do see that the company expanded upon its existing operation with **strategic technology**, for the purpose of delivering a stronger solution for everyday products consumers already valued: in quantity and cheap. As I'm writing this, Sears, once considered utterly unbeatable, has just ended it's 120-year retail run by filing for bankruptcy.

CHAPTER THREE

A NEW APPROACH TO BRANDING PRODUCTS

The most famous story in the history of modern branding is probably the creation of the Citibank logo. The designer, Paula Scher, created the iconic design for the one of the biggest banks in the world on a cocktail napkin, in less than five minutes. The logo, a simple red arch rising over blue text, evokes a fiery sunrise over water, an image which is confident and hopeful. Still in use 25 years later, the logo's origin as a casual ballpoint pen sketch on a cocktail napkin only adds to its power, demonstrating *the ability of even the simplest tools to represent the most complex ideas* - in this case, a 2-trillion-dollar bank.

This story, while inspirational, really exemplifies how companies *used to* think about branding, specifically in eras that pre-date the widespread use of the internet for business and selling. Namely, that **brand content was primarily concerned with communicating the aesthetics, mission, and overall identity of a company**. Before the public adoption of the internet had fully crystallized, branding and logo design were largely synonymous, as logo was the primary form of brand content.

Today, the diversity of brand content which most people experience daily is quite broad. As forms have evolved to include a sophisticated digital palette of copy, image, video, motion graphics, social media, and highly interactive ecommerce experiences, so too has the *purpose* of branding evolved. In their landmark 2002 book, "The Attention Economy," authors Thomas Davenport and John Beck foretold a coming era wherein the currency of businesses would be the amount of attention which consumers gave to an ever-increasing glut of competing online content. This highly prescient view was a major disruption to the "branding as character" model of the past. Now, the purpose of brand content would not be to express "DNA" but to generate *engagement*, as much as possible.

As we enter a new and even more specialized mini-epoch of the digital age - the rise of ecommerce as the dawning central economy of the world - it seems that **this definition of branding needs to be turned on its head again.**

Given that the total output of all internet content is increasingly optimized for some kind of user engagement, it will not be enough for brands to simply "get attention." Can brand elements be used with more specific purpose-oriented goals? **Relative to product, brand *has* to be used in a new way.** If we think of product value as *a uniquely non-commodified customer solution*, and product margin as *the value-add of the company which sells it*, then brand becomes the pillar which holds up both, by "making the case" for both. This utilitarian approach to branding gives it more shape and purpose than the more general role it held in the past. **Today, we can intentionally deploy digital branding concepts and practices for these two specific goals: to *prove* the worth of product *and* to prove the worth of company.**

BRANDING AND NON-COMMODIFICATION

Brand's influence over products can often feel more *magical* than practical. Traditionally, we think of brand as a "voice" with a clear personality, existing only to give products social context and vibe. A unifying aesthetic. A connection to history and culture. A source of humor, color, or comfort. A badge of social proof and a confident call to action. All of these things are still true. But if we don't use the voice of our company to express the value of products in *a solution-oriented way*, the customer is left with no direct reason to engage.

As we have just discussed, product value is a function of how well it solves a customer problem, *plus* how interchangeable that solution may or may not be relative to comparable goods on the market.

Well, probably the simplest way to turn a commodity into a non-commodity is by slapping a logo on it. If non-commodification is about the uniqueness of a solution, logo-oriented branding certainly suggests that "this item, by virtue of the shiny purple sticker we have placed upon it, is unique in all the world." But in order to fully connote value in a crowded marketplace, **that logo must also describe a product solution**.

One of my favorite logos of all time is the Nike swoosh - less so for its aesthetic or culturally ubiquity, and more because of how it has a built-in reference to the *solution* that Nike's products offer. The swoosh evokes an object in motion, producing a wake as it speeds past. This logo does more than just stand out on a crowded shelf - it conveys, in a glance, the nature of the solutions this brand's products will provide: We can help runners run faster. The connection is perhaps growingly abstract relative to this discussion, but it is there - this is branding which supports both uniqueness *and* product solution. You really can't say the same thing for Apple. As famous and iconic as that logo it, it does not speak to solution or price-justification at all.

BRANDING FISH OIL AND FISHERMEN

Walking through the supermarket supplement aisle is an object lesson in brands which transform commodity products into non-commodities, just with what we learn from packaging.

Fish oil is ubiquitous. Sustainably caught organic cold water wild salmon oil from New Zealand is not. Part of that is just product development, but part of it is understanding which elements make this bottle of fish oil a more specific solution over its generic shelf-mates. If as a customer my problem is that I need more omega-3s in my diet, I only trust organic products, I only believe in wild fishing practices, and I have heard that New Zealand is famous for having very clean natural waters, then this product suddenly is very valuable, and worth the extra premium (extra margin) over the generics. The branding elements right on the label, which suggest that this company only produces these types of products, are the proof.

Even if the product itself has no extreme differences from rivals, branding can do much of the heavy lifting just by attitude. Take "Fisherman's Friend," a classic menthol cough drop brand, which uses packaging to liken its customers to rugged seafarers on wooden trawlers in the Atlantic (as opposed to a cubicle jockey with a head cold browsing drugstore analgesics). This product identity, a rugged cough drop for rugged characters, implies a solution. It says, this cough drop will soothe the worst sore throats in the Atlantic, so your land-lubber cough will be no problem at all. If I am looking for the strongest cough drop available, this branding-oriented case will assure me that this product has value for me.

HOW CONTENT SUPPORTS VALUE

Branding in the 21st century is more than just clever packaging or a logo design. "Content" is a broad term to describe the many modern tools there are to *express* a brand's take on its product, its customer, and itself. Slogans, product descriptions, blogs, social posts, videos, apps, in-store displays, it's all fair game. Is a 6-lb. paper Sears Catalog content? Yes. Is a pic posted to Snapchat content? Yes. Is a spam text to your phone offering to sell you real estate content? Yes. All forms of media, invented or not-yet-invented, which humans and businesses use to communicate, is content.

No matter the form, content's primary practical function is now to **support the value of the product by explaining the solution it provides to the customer.** Whether or not content literally enumerates a series of benefits for the customer, in a larger sense, each piece of content should be used to create the *idea* of value.

If out of 3.5 billion internet users, 300 million of them are logging onto Twitter every month, it is certainly worthwhile for a brand to speak on the platform. But unless those tweets are furthering the goal of *demonstrating product solutions*, they are at risk of becoming part of the noise around a brand which actually *gets in the way* of suggesting value. If Nissan tweets about the growing number of charging stations in America, it is solving its specific customer problem of "It is not easy to find charging stations for electric cars (including the Nissan Leaf)." That's the basis for a terrific tweet, even if it does not directly mention the Nissan product. It doesn't need to. If instead, Nissan tweets a photograph of the new plant where its electric cars are produced, while of interest to fans, there is no real effect upon the perceived value of those cars.

So some good questions to ask relative to brand content are these: how can I use this format to define what this brand solves for customers? How can I express attributes in the form of *benefits*? What's the core lifestyle issue which this product addresses? How does it feel to use it? How does it bring relief? If you want to talk about price, even this can be expressed as a customer solution/benefit. The point is that everything the brand says is bringing the customer closer to their answers. *What will solve my problem? Why is this solution worth its price?*

Content itself is *not* a conversion-driver. It simply expresses the solution.

The *solution* which your product offers is the *only* real conversion-driver. Content's role is to express that solution. The art of content creation is in the creativity and precision with which you deliver that message. Every single thing that content expresses must pertain to how this product gets us closer to the solution the customer seeks.

Benefits. Reasons. Proof of specific value. That's the formula, and once you know that, it makes it easier to figure out how to speak in these venues in ways which will resonate. In this way, the content always addresses the direct pain point of the consumer, and suggests that **the solution to that pain point lies in acquiring the product**.

Content is *evidence*.
It's all of the information which builds the argument for the product's value.

Bad content misunderstands a customer's goals. Bad content misunderstands a product's exact role in those goals. However, content which answers customer pain points in an abstract/artful way is not automatically bad content. If you want to answer a customer pain point of *"how do I reduce stress?"* with an image of an attractive couple lying on a beach drinking a beer, with no copy, no explanation, no url, that's still fantastic content because it does directly address what the customer is looking for. (Let's say for this example that you are selling the beer.)

The "bad content" version of the same ad might feature a famous rock star drinking a beer. Yes, many ads feature celebrities holding branded merchandise, but in this case *"famous people love it"* does not answer the consumer's need to alleviate stress, at all. No matter how beautifully the image was shot or how expensive the celebrity was to hire, this was a wasted opportunity. However, in deference to Kylie Jenner fans, I'll qualify that - if the customer problem is "how can I be more like celebrities?" then the ad works.

BRANDING AND MARGIN

The other half of branding's role is to describe this same kind of solution and benefit-oriented message, but for the value which the brand offers *in addition* to the product itself. In a sense, we're **proving the value of the company**, compared to anyone else who might be offering something similar. The point of this is to **justify the margin** - what we're asking *above* the value of the product. How does your brand - its services, shopping experience, reputation, mission, and communication - add **solution-oriented value** to the products you sell?

Think of branding as "making the case" *for your margins.*

This is a great way look at it - setting "margin's case" as the goal is a lot more effective than a more generalized branding objective like "make us look cool," "compete with big box retail," or even just "get more conversions." How do you use brand to get more conversions? That's a tough topic to approach. But "building a case for margins" is very specific and the right launching point for brand strategy.

"Not only" is a great tool for this kind of branding. *Not only* does this car get incredible mileage, but you can pre-select all of your options online and be out the door with your new ride in half the time. *Not only* is this beard oil the answer to dry skin, but you can easily exchange it if you don't like the smell. *Not only* do we make a world class ecommerce platform, but we're also really fun to work with. **First the value of the product, then the value of the company.**

This isn't really about sloganeering, but the *ethos* of a brand. It can be expressed in other ways than just words. But what these ideas are saying is, "in addition to offering a valuable product, *the way we offer it* is worth a lot."

Here's a homework assignment: search for athletic socks on Amazon. Between items from a well-known brand such as Under Armour, vs. a nearly identical-looking international knock-off version with an unrecognizable brand which sells for a dollar less, which do you choose, and why?

BRAND VS. PRODUCT FRICTION

Finally, we want to look at branding as it works with friction around products. In this context, **"friction" is hassle**. It's any inconvenience. It's any slow-down. It's any cumbersome process or person. It's anything which gets between a customer and their solution. Friction can be enormous, or it can be tiny. In all cases, friction is the enemy of value and margin. High friction means that this is not the easiest solution around. Customers, burned many times over the years by inferior experiences, are often wary when approaching a new online seller ... *is this going to be easier than just buying the thing on Amazon?* Of course we want to use every tool at hand to reduce any and all friction, more on that later, but as we build a case for the value of our products, we want to use the brand to communicate how little friction exists around it. In this way, **brand also "makes the case" for how *friction-free* dealing with its products is.**

The classic example of a high-friction experience around purchasing a specific product would be buying clothing. Clothes were initially slow to take off online for this very reason - sizing, delivery, and most importantly, returns, could often be annoyingly inefficient in the early days of ecommerce.

Apparel is a huge industry - it's generally the largest non-housing expense for most households after groceries and healthcare. Even bigger than transportation for most people. Obviously ecommerce was ripe for apparel and apparel was ripe for ecommerce, but there was a stumble to get going because the return rates for apparel companies are usually around 30 percent or more - and this was a huge source of friction online. In the beginning customers had to call online sellers and ask for a return verbally, and the customer service rep would try to determine whether or not to grant it, almost like a negotiation to return or not. And then they had to figure out how to get you the label to send it back, and then you had to go drop it off at post office. **These annoying extra steps were a huge impediment to sales growth.**

Obviously today it's very common that when you order apparel online, it arrives with a return shipping label and a policy of no-questions-asked returns. Sellers realized a long time ago that it's just better to take all returns regardless and sort out fraud another way, than it is to have to pay workers to talk on the phone to customers about every return. This strategy, though, led to even more friction problems.

Originally, if a company printed a label for a customer return, they'd pay for the shipping immediately, whether or not a customer actually mailed back the item. This meant that companies could not pre-manage returns without incurring tons of unnecessary charges. Eventually, shipping companies created API infrastructure which now allows sellers to print a return label and include it in the package, and it doesn't cost anything. Sellers only pay for the shipping if the item actually gets returned. One by one, other friction-reducing aspects were figured out, for example, how to economically vary the shipping speed of those returns compared to outgoing shipments of orders, which need to move much faster. Finally, other front end elements like sizing charts, body type charts, etc., help people figure out in advance if something's going to fit, which head off the problem of the return before the sale is even made. The combined result was new operational efficiency around apparel returns. **Removing friction around the return allowed apparel ecommerce to flourish.**

Quickly, **a brand's ability to articulate how little friction there was around its products became a key component of all messaging**, and a powerful way to let brand support margin. The phrase "hassle-free returns" is an example of brand content which describes friction-reduction, and uses it to make the case for shopping with a particular vendor.

A WEB OF TOUCH POINTS

The amount of hassle your customer has to endure around every single interaction with your product is often a deciding factor in their perceptions and purchases going forward. We'll dive deeper into how to nuke friction from the overall online shopping experience in the following several chapters, but as we conclude the discussion of products, start to think about the web of emotional experiences which fan out from the product and touch the customer's life.

"Touch points" are a constellation of brand interactions that a shopper experiences over their total life cycle with the product. Some common ones are product discovery, shopping experience, fulfilment, product use, customer service, ongoing marketing, and end of product use.

At each point along the way, what is your customer is feeling? Is this part of the process easy or hard? Does each phase bring your customer closer to their goal or further away? Does each point of contact speed up their relief or slow it down?

Or, did some of the touch points **create more friction than they needed to**? Was the discovery process cumbersome? Was it to hard to find good information about the product? Where did they view your site and how did the product look when displayed? Did the product ship in a timely manner relative to the customer's goal? Did the product deliver the benefits that were promised? Did all communications from the brand, such as marketing emails, support the concept of the solution offered? Was customer service also oriented this way, structured to deliver the most friction-free answer possible?

Just asking these questions is usually a huge help. It allows us to see the product *as the customer sees it*. More importantly, it allows us to zero in on any parts of the process which are not supporting product value. By keeping our heads around the product, the "esoteric" art of branding becomes practical - **how is my brand helping or hindering my ability to give the customer what they want?**

No matter what size business you are, today the tools exist to dig in and reduce the friction around every touch point. Your attention to reducing hassle **aligns brand goal with customer goal** - both sides want exactly the same thing! That alignment is the factor which adds *humanity* to your brand. Real people are going through this experience that you've created... always strive to be a part of the solution to their problems, while reducing any additional stress you might be adding to the equation.

This idea of using friction reduction to support customers is what I call "**humanity branding**." Examine every point of friction around the product, and de-frictionize, by adding compassionate, empathetic support. *How does this feel? What does this inspire? Why is this frustrating? How could this be faster, more relevant, more fun?* Then, as with the other aspects of product value which we've discussed, you have to talk about it, and often.

We want to stay pinpoint-focused on how the product, experience, and information we provide gets customers closer to their goals. This is the way we instill our products with value, it's the way we should be using our brands, and it's the way we ultimately thrive. That's why your job isn't to "defeat" trillion dollar multi-national corporations. **Your job is to solve pain, and let the world know what that solution is worth.**

PART II: PLATFORM

When I was in college, many of the biggest tech companies in today's world were either struggling to survive amidst a coming epoch-change, or they didn't exist at all. The term "FAANG stocks" had not yet been created. In the retail space, the types of technology used by rising talents were still largely physical - innovations revolved around coordinating physical stores with physical supply chain mastery. Mass media systems for marketing were non-interactive, and only personalized in the most rudimentary sense - if you watched the ABC sitcom "Home Improvement," for example, you'd be shown a series of 30-second ads which only loosely targeted the audience's family demographics - aspirin, mattresses, fast food, etc.

But something new was clearly on the horizon, and approaching fast. There was a very real sense that personal computing was opening up to uses beyond local gaming, word processing and document management, as CompuServe, Prodigy, AOL, et al were starting to introduce the concepts of chat, online forums, news, and basic shopping. Students at my university were beginning to use "electronic mail" to converse with students at other schools. The zesty thought at the time was, what if *everybody* was on the World Wide Web? What if *everything* was linked? The push was to subvert outdated, physical modes of communication, and bring everyone onto the same, unified "superhighway." That was the meaning of *disrupt,* then: bring all of these separate entities *together* with technology.

Now, just a couple of decades later, what it means to "buck the status quo" has completely reversed. As a handful of mega-corporations consolidated the movement of information across the internet, the way to be revolutionary was to *separate* from the pack, to create and maintain independence.... *Keep my data private. Let me be the ultimate curator of all content that passes before me. Run my store by my rules.* Ecommerce, which had already been born, bubbled, crashed, rebuilt, and risen to dominance in those same decades, developed basic models for selling which allowed masses of self-determining businesses to prosper on every scale. They were de facto islands, running upstart shops that competed with the titans and every now and then become them.

Today, I see that we are moving out of this second phase of staunch independence, and into something new: the era of **"complete ecom-**

merce." In this new reality, smart software will enable the best of all worlds: *utter integration* among providers, sellers, and shoppers, at the same time as *utter personalization* dialed in to each and every unique business and shopper. Now, it turns out that being a disrupter means embracing the best of our *shared* digital experience, while simultaneously *customizing* our journey through it down to the pixel. That's the idea behind today's complete ecommerce - total unity, *and* total independence.

CHAPTER FOUR

COMPLETE ECOMMERCE

MINIMUM VERSUS MAXIMUM

Reminiscing about the early days of ecommerce, it's incredible how *little* we asked of it then, yet how unfathomably *enormous* the whole idea felt at the time. The gold rush leading into the dotcom bubble had turned everyone into a cunning ecommerce expert overnight. Suddenly anyone with a GeoCities account and a credit card was making plans for their personal global sales empire, and investors were tripping over one another to sink billions into the opportunity of a lifetime.

Ambitions aside, the early ecommerce sites were little more than simple databases of products, with very basic transactions and a chaos of inconsistent design standards. The concept of "shopping experience" had not really been articulated yet - but most consumers who shopped online prior to 2000 were buoyed by the novelty of being an early adopter of something *so* revolutionary. Do you remember your first online purchase? It felt somewhat miraculous when the thing would actually show up, didn't it? Like you had somehow gamed the system and used the cheat codes at the very edge of human innovation, as you opened your box containing a hardcover copy of "Harry Potter and the Chamber of Secrets," then exclaimed to anyone who'd listen, "I bought it on the internet!"

Even now, we are still in the infancy of what ecommerce will become. We're not even a toddler. So it's mindblowing to try to imagine what the state of ecommerce was like before the world had really conceived of the elaborate, deeply complex data systems which are now so sophisticated/automated/intuitive that they are largely invisible to the businesses which use them every day. Yet, the majority of our industry is still trying to "make it work" with cookie cutter, one-size-fits-all ecommerce software which is not all that different from those basic homepage-product-page-checkout sites of yore.

I refer to this stuck-in-retro phenomenon as **"Minimum Viable Ecommerce."** "Minimum viable" is frequently used to describe products or business models which can sustain *rudimentary* functionality. It's an apt metaphor for the state of legacy ecommerce software, which our industry is clearly moving away from. Because now we can do so much more than "get a product on the shelf, take money for it, and ship it out the door," which is pretty much the *mission statement* for minimum viable ecommerce. But still, there is tension around whether, collectively, we should be striving for more ease/uniformity, or more complexity/customization. This question is at the heart of a "protective" Amazon strategy, not to mention why Amazon has become what it's become, and I think it bears diving into in some more detail.

In "minimum viable ecommerce," businesses must *reduce* the complexity of their operations and strategy *down* to the limitations of generic software.

The dotcom crash began in the spring of 2000 and claimed at least half of the world's ecommerce projects, which were in various stages of untested concepts, impractical use cases, unsustainable burn rates, p.r. disasters, and investor revolts. This moment acted like a digital forest fire, clearing out vaporware dreams which existed only in whitepapers, and prepared a new playing field for a wide range of real, functional online businesses. For every govWorks.com (the doomed subject of the dotcom bubble documentary "Startup.com"), there were thousands of stripped-down ecommerce sites ready to launch. Coming from the inflection point of the crash, a new world of minimally viable ecommerce was a dream to reach for. Systems that *simply worked* at all would be enough.

Expedia, Zappos, Barnes and Noble, Staples, and Target, all launched limited ecommerce sites towards the end of the 90s, and for the big companies with major resources, dividing up the then-incredible 13 billion in annual online retail sales was a sweet deal. (For reference, today we are above 400 billion per year.)

If this industry was going to endure and open up to more than just 10 mega-brands, developers would have to **apply technology to solve for the problem of bloated concepts and management software that couldn't really manage anything.** Accessible ecommerce solutions would have to go beyond the hobbyist home business run out of the garage on weekends, and tackle the realities of physically *and* digitally moving goods and resources through a complicated supply chain from factory to front door.

This idea would evolve into what we today think of as "complete ecommerce" - custom-built interfaces capable of seamlessly managing even the most complex multi-national brand machines and the goods they sell, to highly diverse groups of individual and B2B shoppers.

In "complete ecommerce," software systems adapt and expand to support the processes and goals of the business.

We've come a long way since the bubble burst and a modern industry was born in its wake. But unless businesses are aware of and take steps to implement systems which drive them to the maximum, rather than just help them *get by* with the minimum, I'm afraid that most will suffer the same fate as those over-ambitious speculators from two decades ago.

THE ORIGINAL ECOMMERCE SITES

The original ecommerce sites were set up almost like a library. Think about the traditional library model - you're scanning through piles of little information cards to find something, and you have to know precisely what you're looking for, or at least the standardized topic of what you're looking for. From there you go through a process of... unraveling. Hunting, and hoping.

In early online shopping, there was a category or categorical hierarchy of products, which shoppers researched through, to ultimately discover whatever thing that they wanted. The web was slow. Sellers couldn't use the kind of photography being used today because the file sizes would have been absolutely enormous and unsupportable (see also: history of data compression). Picture quality was low, detailed product information was scarce, and customers had real "risk" concerns about credit card use. Ironically, back then, a typical shopper's fraud concern wasn't around hackers stealing credit cards, the concern was that the person who put the site up was just going to take that credit card and do something nefarious with it. There simply wasn't any basis of trust. The experience was still pretty rough from 1996 on, but it was the beginning of a long maturation period.

Soon, ecommerce will be divided into those who leverage technology to highlight the real value for their products and real solutions for their customers, vs. those who kill time "getting by" while the majority of minimum viable ecommerce sellers move (as they probably should) to Amazon.

This again gets to **the central question for ecommerce disrupters** looking to upend the status quo: how can we strive toward more specialization, without returning to the laborious bog of non-functioning sites which companies like Shopify and Amazon "solved" by narrowing choices to the lowest common denominator?

THE "MASTER'S TOOLS"

Masters in every field - be they mechanics, programmers, or great chefs - all have one thing in common: *they use highly specialized tools.* Imagine a master artisan sculpting a clay bust by hand. She uses a sophisticated and well-established collection of tools to scrape, smooth, and shape, she turns the clay on a sculpting wheel, and in this era, she uses 3D modeling software to develop her designs digitally. Without the proper implements to make it a reality, ideas would remain locked in the sculptor's head.

This is not limited to the creation of art. Within the software that has been designed specifically to manage business processes, a master artisan is *defined* by the tools they use. "I'm a Python coder" is a completely different artist than "I'm a Photoshop designer," but each is intrinsically defined by their tool of choice.

Most ecommerce platforms today are still like a Swiss army knife - a collection of small, general tools adapted to small tasks. A Swiss army knife is useful if you want to open a small package, file your nails, or scale a sunfish. However you probably wouldn't get very far if you tried to use one to build a 2-stage rocket capable of safely hauling 60 tons of cargo into space.

Maybe that example is a little extreme. But **no master of any field would attempt to execute professional work with tools that were ill-equipped to do the task before them.** It is the sophistication of the tool and people's dexterity with it that combine to create mastery. Without the tool, the master is simply an intellectual, with no practical ability to execute their plans. With the wrong tool, makeshift fixes to complicated problems doom projects to failure.

Probably the broadest, most relatable example of "the master's tools" in ecommerce is certainly going to come from, at some level, the nemesis of this book, Amazon. Amazon has mastered what I would argue are the most ridiculously complex tasks in ecommerce - logistics, delivery, and returns. They have been able to make virtually every product in this country exist "within two days" of virtually all people. They have achieved this with the ultimate master's tools, which in their case are very talented software coders who can basically write *anything* from scratch.

Slightly smaller businesses can also manage complexity in this way. In the early days of Zappos, for example, when the company had maybe 100 - 200 employees, they were the first to solve the apparel ecommerce-specific problem of trying on and returning shoes. Zappos knew full well that a third or more of the shoes that they shipped out were going to come back. They needed systems for letting people return them. They needed systems for once shoes got back to the warehouse, to inspect them. And then they needed systems to package these shoes for resale. These are complicated tasks that cry out for the master's tools.

From the customer's perspective, **application of the master's tools leads to shopping experiences that have less and less friction**. From the business' perspective, more specialized tools minimize friction around whatever selling modality they want to achieve. So, in the case of, say, returning a pair of shoes, if the way the shipping box was engineered is such that the customer can put those same shoes back in the same box and attach the pre-printed label that came with it, neither party is hassled unnecessarily.

THE PLATFORM

In this discussion, the ultimate master's tool that we're talking about is **the ecommerce platform**. Think of an ecommerce platform as a sculpting tool that comes in many shapes and sizes - the one you select to pull from the drawer and build your masterpiece with will play a role in the scope and complexity of work you are able to create.

Stunning advances in UX design have made modern ecommerce storefronts feel more like wandering through 3D art installations, but the fact remains: your **site** is only an external, non-physical *representation* of your business. The site is a portal of communication between customer and the seller. It is not the business itself, nor is it what businesses are purchasing when they shop for ecommerce software. Most laymen don't actually make this distinction, a general confusion which is encouraged by the wave of pop DIY services like Squarespace, and WordPress before it.

The ecommerce *platform* is the tool we use to create the site, but this definition is also somewhat limiting and needs to be challenged. Can we imagine that an ecommerce platform is more like a sort of train station, through which every possible bit of data connected to a business can flow in and out. The purpose of guiding all data streams through a central "station" is obvious: **all systems within a business' total ecosystem are interdependent** - the more information they have about the status of every other system, the more capable they are at executing the tasks put to them. Human tasks, and those run by a piece of code. Public-facing and back of the house. The platform in a sense "projects" the site out to the world, but this is only one of its key functions. That's another important point, because what we really want to do is start looking at this type of system as a *communication* medium, more than just as a selling medium.

The ecommerce *solution* is the sum of all software, systems, and human strategy which comprise a business, including the people who run it and the people who buy from it. "Tech world" has been in love with this term from time immemorial, at times obnoxiously so, but in ecommerce, "solution" takes on another layer of meaning which is highly relevant. I like this word here, because when it's used in ecommerce it connects the processes of a business with its purpose: *solving customer needs.* As discussed in the last section, we also see products as solutions. Well, the "ecommerce solution" links the answer to the customer's problem with the answer to the business' problem. This is a helpful concept.

It's easy to get a little lost in the weeds when discussing these various non-physical concepts. But this kind of thinking, about *solutions* rather than just *sites*, does powerfully align the needs of the business with those of the customer. It is the beginning of "complete ecommerce" thinking, and it's a crucial bit of understanding needed to protect an independent ecommerce business' role in any selling process.

If minimum viable ecommerce asks, "*how can I display these products and take money for them?,*" complete ecommerce asks, **"how can I solve for the interconnected pain points of my business and its customers?"** That's a huge difference, and really helps explain *why* we need the master's tools. These tools have been honed, tested, revised, and improved collectively over 25 million ecommerce stores. We now know what works, and what breaks under pressure. The purpose of all of it is a better solution for all, an overall experience with less friction, and better answers.

A complete ecommerce solution's main goal is to *reduce friction* for buyer and seller.

LEANING UP OPERATIONS

There is a lot to consider at the outset of an ecommerce project. It's really like directing a 200-million dollar action film - there are so many perspectives to consider, no matter how big or small the business is. Your retail customer says, "I want a site that is as dialed in as possible to exactly what I am looking for." Your B2B customer says, "don't waste my time with too many steps and clicks." Your community says, "give us bright and bold creative, with a place to get questions answered and tell the world what we think." Your IT department says, "failsafe backups and no downtime please." Your sales department says, "let us streamline quotes, accounts, and prefs on a case by case basis." Your customer service team says, "can we build in enough self-service to reduce the number of open tickets?" Your marketing director says, "is it easy to integrate site content, email campaigns, and SEO best practices?" Your social media manager says, "can we set an auto feed from Instagram?" Your warehouse says, "can we digitize our inventory and automate most of fulfilment?" Your COO says, "can we link the data streams from ERP to orders to analytics and back again?" Your CEO says, "ROI."

It's a mouthful. When trying to juggle a list like this, "disrupt" can be the first casualty - you're just trying to keep all of those balls in the air. I have found it helpful to keep coming back to the idea of solution, which really means "relief." What actions here will reduce stress, alleviate uncertainty, and free up mindspace to do good work? This is what all of those voices are asking for. Relief.

The development of increasingly specialized ecommerce software has enabled the "leaning up" of businesses - meaning much smaller teams can manage much bigger operations. You're going to find that these tools have allowed for people to have very discrete and focused roles. So not only are the teams smaller, but there is less need for each worker to be a "jack of all trades." The software carries that burden. By fulfilling each department's efficiency requests, individuals are freed up to focus with more specificity. At the head of the organization, the business owner or executive is freed up to skip the small stuff and simply *direct*.

Let's say I have a website, I have orders coming in, and I want my fulfillment person to go grab items from the warehouse and ship them out. A logistical issue might be that 70 percent of the items I shipped are in my warehouse, 30 percent are shipped by fulfillment center. This would be a massive headache and time-filler for humans to sort out. And so our tools and technologies can be purposed for the routing and automation of those complex tasks to happen before they even reach the team members. If I'm that fulfillment person, all the key decisions have already been made for me. The correctly-sized box I need should be ready, labels should be printed and waiting, the locations in the warehouse where the items are should be predetermined. My job then becomes helping get these things out the door in a safe manner.

The upshot is that **this business does not need an arsenal of managers to plan every line item of this operation**, it doesn't need a warehouse worker to also be a transit logistics maestro, and it doesn't require the owner to be standing over the shoulder of their workers making sure all of these non-creative decisions are sound.

IS AUTOMATION THE ENEMY OF HUMAN ACHIEVEMENT?

So much of what we do online today used to be done by people literally calling other people, and now, those tasks have turned into APIs and middleware and programs talking to APIs. Is this progress? For me, this type of automation is very positive, simply because *humans don't make great computers*. Humans are great problem solvers, but are not as ideal at exacting repetitive tasks which don't require any creative thinking.

In the early days of ecommerce, one of the pioneering developers that we worked with in the Miva community was Jeff Collins, a very talented ecommerce developer who created a project called florist.com, which would eventually be bought out by FTD. At the beginning, Jeff was trying to solve core friction issues for this industry, such as delivery windows. If an order comes in online and someone needs it tomorrow, how do you get it routed so that the correct local team can fulfill the highly time-sensitive order? In this case the pressure for maximum efficiency was very pronounced: flowers wilt.

Originally, long distance floral delivery worked by largely physical connections. You might walk into a local flower shop, and “send” a dozen roses across the country. This was achieved by a sales clerk manually researching and calling a shop at the local destination, who would then arrange delivery. Now we essentially have algorithms which handle almost every part of that task, fairly invisibly.

Today we see new crop of ecommerce-enabled flower sellers which actually grow their own products, perhaps internationally, and then ship directly all around the world because logistics have gotten so fast and manageable. But, back in 1998, shipping directly from Costa Rica to anywhere in the world wasn’t a viable option for a business. And so florist.com was customized to map to the network of available local vendors all across the country. What used to rely on telephones and humans was solved by pioneers like Jeff in a non-cookie cutter way.

When the core decisions are algorithmically generated, perhaps a combination of distance/stock/price, etc., there is no need for the creative power of the human brain working the problem. By taking the human guesswork out of choosing among various local vendors, the algorithm provides the most consistent results and therefore the most consistent customer experience.

If you’re feeling anxiety about how that type of automation has cost an army of phone operators their livelihood, you could just compare the yearly revenue of florist.com in 1999 versus ftd.com today, which clocked a billion dollars in orders in 2017. **How much more opportunity was created by this growth, for workers and customers alike?**

I think there are ultimately two things that come out of the automation process. One is that automation usually reduces the price to consumers. Especially in a market that’s competitive. You get more flowers today for your dollar than you did back when there were humans involved because these companies are far leaner and far more precise.

The bigger philosophical answer is, historically speaking, disrupting and automating human tasks has led to greater and greater progress for all of humanity. Back in the 18th century, the great majority of human work effort went to producing food. Let's say 90% or more. Today, automated systems for farming, preparing, packaging, and distributing food means that only two or three percent of human labor now goes to producing food. The rest of our collective time can be put to other purposes, other innovations - like designing the perfect system to get your sweetheart that bouquet of flowers on their birthday.

We need to free people up from doing mundane tasks which computers are good at, so that we can be creative about more complex and creative problems.

A SOLUTION FOR EVERY PROBLEM

The feature set for a enterprise-level ecommerce platform should be intimidatingly long. But if there is not a real *solution* attached to a feature, it is just window dressing. It's great for a platform to offer a feature like responsive frameworks keyed to different kinds of devices, but you need to know *why* - in this case, because *customers need platforms that adapt to their behavior and aren't rigid.* Now that feature has value.

Overall, operations from inventory to orders to shipping need to be as streamlined as possible - too many cooks required for every tiny task is a drag on everyone, so we want to solve for a host of inefficiencies and liberate those teams. But there must always be an end solution in mind, otherwise we are just tricking out an economy car with $50,000 rims for our daily commute to work.

Customization of features is the key - and customization with intention. Whether we are talking about content creation, order tracking and fulfilment, warehouse efficiency, payment integration, pricing and couponing, accounts, security protections, the list goes on and on... the more each feature can be customized, the more it will all "just work" for any given business.

Minimum viable ecommerce platforms hype the appeal of slick site templates and long lists of entry-level bells and whistles to obscure the real issue: **non-customized ecommerce sites have such generalized/limited functionality that they are not a perfect fit for *any* business.**

In this industry, there is no end to "innovation for innovation's sake" - meaning, a marketing calendar dictates X number of new features released per quarter. But these releases are incomplete if they are not driven by very specific customer solutions. It is better to start with a clear idea of those questions for an individual business, and then seek out the appropriate features, rather than trying to wedge in every new release into every site.

As a provider of these features, with a floor full of developers busting tail to innovate new answers every day, the guiding principle for me, same as for my customers, is always going to be *how does this more directly solve this specific problem?* "Augmented Reality ecommerce is trending on Recode" is not a great reason to develop or implement AR for an ecommerce app. "My customers primarily use their phones to shop my home furnishing products, but they are desperate for a solution which allows them to visualize our dining room tables in their own homes" is a brilliant reason to discuss AR. It's not just semantics. I'm talking about moving with purpose and letting go of all the other noise.

AMAZON AS A PLATFORM

Is Amazon just a very large ecommerce platform? There is a mental tendency to categorize marketplaces as "service providers," akin to UPS, etc. But let's remember what Amazon actually is, because it will be instructive to see it relative to our own businesses. It hosts products, acts as distributor for other manufacturers, handles accounts, fulfilment, customer service, it markets itself on-site and offers streamlined transactions and payment. This sure sounds like an ecommerce platform.

That begs another question: **If Amazon is an ecommerce platform, is it more in the "master artisan" category or is it a**

"cookie cutter"?

Though there have been many evolutions of the Amazon site's look and feel over the years, the essential shopping experience has remained the same. Scanning through product pages and search results, it certainly *feels* like minimum viable ecommerce, doesn't it? Certainly from a user standpoint. Every layout is from the same template. Every product has the same simple presentation of attributes. Overall, Amazon behaves the same whether a user is buying 1 widget or 100, whether they drive a Honda or a Ford, whether it's their first purchase or 1000th. We extrapolate that the seller end of that experience is equally stripped down and generalized. What we must conclude is this:

Customization (or lack thereof) is the key difference between "minimum viable" and "complete" ecommerce.

The greater the degree of customization your ecommerce platform has, the greater your advantage is over cookie cutter solutions selling your same product (or product category), *including* Amazon. So, more customization, or more of the ability to customize, is further protection against Amazon.

The world is moving towards more specialization, more customization... not less. If you can embrace this, your ecommerce platform itself can become your competitive advantage over rivals. What I mean by this is, **the way you sell is as important as what you sell**.

CHAPTER FIVE

INTEGRATIONS MATTER

It wasn't that long ago, as recently as the early 1990s, that the only way to effectively do work on a computer was to literally be at your office. A small subset of professional workers around that time were early adopters of a new and exciting device called a "laptop." This was before we even used the word "device" to identify computing gear. My first laptop was a giant, cumbersome thing which weighed 10 pounds and cost $12,000 to buy. I felt rather proud of this machine, as there was still a vague social connotation that one's work had to be valuable enough to justify such an extravagance. I could go home, dial into my corporate network, and in a *very* slow fashion, get some work done. This was truly living large! And it was a great early example of how integrated systems support and expand the efficiency - and *pain relief* - of doing business. As a businessman, mobile access to work communications means I can offer my customers and team members round-the-clock service and support. The reach of my business is extended across time and space, well beyond what I could practically achieve by sitting in an office chair shackled to a desktop. This heightened efficiency means that my company is more efficient, more helpful. Ergo, our services become more valuable to our clients. If my personal pain point is "I need more flexible work hours to improve my quality of life," then this big old laptop from 1992 solved that - suddenly I don't have to go in to work on a Saturday to fix some small but urgent crisis. I have time to enjoy my coffee, pet my dog, and set priorities for my time that don't always align with a traditional 40-hour work week. By simply linking ubiquitous tools like a laptop, a Wi-Fi network, an email client, and various encryption protections, I am able to fundamentally change and improve how I work. That's an integration, and it's one that we now all know so intimately that it's invisible.

Many people today, if their management systems are in place, can work from a laptop, tablet, or phone, from almost anywhere. That's easy. But ideas like this have set the stage for the more advanced systems integrations which now fuel complete ecommerce. The core concept is still the same: **integrations with several small, specialized systems increase the power, reach, and value of the whole.**

"CUSTOM" MEANS UNIQUELY INTEGRATED

Yes, anyone can still launch a store with a template, a PayPal account, and a handful of simple products that can be wedged into a pre-set navigation. But for building businesses which can scale sustainably, it becomes more and more important to look behind the storefront for ways to enhance the overall value of the services provided.

Meaningfully linking a custom array of standalone software systems to the center of operations is "integration" in the most basic terms: getting the most out of every tool available by linking those tools, and empowering them to empower one another.

We could describe the ecommerce platform as **a universal translator** - the central communication hub for all aspects of your business - physical and non-physical, financial and non-financial, employee, executive, and customer. Now, what happens if that translator doesn't speak the "local languages" of all those disparate entities? Your ecommerce platform is suddenly a *barrier* to the flow of data, and that means weaker, less-informed solutions.

In a larger sense, it's easy to understand that a shopping experience which is built so broadly that it accommodates a vast number of different business models will not perform as well as one that was built specifically for an individual business. That's the trade off. Entry-level platforms are cheaper (at first) than custom builds because they are built for the many. Basic ecommerce platforms don't really speak "the local languages" anywhere, they just stand on the corner and point at things, hoping enough tourists will know which way to go. This method can work if you are a starter seller, beginning a small business with a handful of products that you want to test, refine, and develop over time. There is nothing wrong with that - many legendary businesses start as a simple idea in someone's garage. However, keep in mind that the moment that hypothetical business in the garage connects to the right audience with the right products and starts to scale up, it will promptly start shopping for a new custom ecommerce solution which can adapt to the developing conditions. As it should.

The more integrated your business is with the services which support it, the better those services can perform, and the more value you can offer your customers.

"Custom" in an ecommerce context is not the same as adding a spoiler to a sports car only because it completes the look. It is a good metaphor though, if the spoiler is added to reduce turbulence which is lowering the performance of the car. What I'm getting at is, just like with products, decisions about how to beef up the sophistication of an ecommerce solution should be driven by solution-thinking. *What problem does this solve?* That's a lot more helpful than the similar but less effective "wouldn't this be cool?"

Every business has unique problems to solve for its customers, and as such each one needs to rely on a different set of support systems. To get the most out of those systems, they must be precision-linked to data flows emanating from ecommerce operations. So for example, tethering an automated email marketing system to on-site order behavior like abandoned carts is useful because it saves worker time and re-connects customers with purchases they may have had trouble completing. That's two problems solved. A different company may find that its customers don't prioritize email and prefer to receive offers over social media, so an integration of retargeted product feeds to Facebook carousel ads would be a better integration. Why not "los dos"? Sure. But again, more specific solutions are obviously better than more generic "catch-all" ones. We often think of "custom" as discretionary, or a wasteful luxury - but in ecommerce platform builds, **it just means arranging specific tools in a unique way, with intention.** Neither option is possible from a marketplace, and so clearly that's money left on the table... it's also an example of your customers not getting served as well by the dragon as they might be by you.

BIG DATA & ECOMMERCE

There are some significant studies brewing which suggest that gross margins for retailers have begun to decline since the mass adoption of Amazon for retail shopping. It's estimated that the top 10 U.S. retail businesses may have experienced a more than 10 percent dip in gross margins since 2010 - while Amazon has experienced growth of gross margins by that same amount or more.

The most obvious reason for this is that more people are finding more cost-effective solutions on Amazon - and retailers are slashing prices to compete. But I do not think that price competition is the real story here. This is a story about effective integration, and specifically the use of data to fuel it. **The antidote is not more aggressive discounts, but more effective solutions.** To do this, we must integrate that data between stores, 3rd party software, and real-world workflows. We must continually leverage data into a tool.

The term "big data" is frequently used as a pejorative at the moment. The New York Times reports that behavioral scientists have cracked a code which uses innocuous Facebook likes to predict personality traits. With 300 likes over the course of one's entire Facebook career, personality can be identified with more accuracy than by one's own spouse. The capture, interpretation, and sale of this kind of data analysis has become insanely controversial on every front: personal, professional, political.

When social media first hit, we were all marking things somewhat innocently, such as "I like The Smiths," or "I like The Big Lebowski." We weren't expecting that to be used to predict what products we would buy for the next 20 years, which candidates we would vote for, which content we should be shown. Our collective sheepishness about the role of this data in modern life now is entirely justified, as challenging conversations about our data are really *just* getting underway for our society as a whole.

A lot of people think of data, or more specifically the collection and implementation of consumer internet data, as a dragon that is swooping in to diminish the freedom and flexibility of independent businesses and consumers. The fear is that this data will be wielded by enormous entities like Microsoft, Google, or Amazon to control our total journeys across the internet, including where and how we shop. The raging **net neutrality** debate questions whether the internet itself is a utility like power or water, which should have built-in protections for users to shop and browse without limits. And the ongoing cultural crisis over Facebook's use of personal data to fuel a 40-billion-dollar/year advertising empire has significantly eroded public trust in all kinds of online data management.

The fallout from this moment could be yet another squeezing out of smaller businesses' ability to compete with Amazon, or more likely, that customers will simply get worse experiences. Not because the FCC limits which data goes where, but as the public increasingly sours on offering up its own data, independent sellers will have less and less information which helps them serve those customers. This is the balance that will have to be struck with data privacy. All data collection is not obtrusive, spying, or manipulative.

Sometimes the Orwellian qualities of the debate do sound quite chilling. By the time they are well into adulthood, today's children will carry with them a record of every website they ever visited, every product they bought, every product they browsed. But as our collective ability to capture, store, and interpret the data of everyday life matures, our ability to interact with one another through that data will also (hopefully) mature. It will be up to all of us to figure out how to use that data responsibly and effectively, if we use it at all. But be sure of this: today's battles over data and privacy are just the very earliest foreshock to the massive questions we will have to address in the future, when there may be profound changes to how we view a subject like privacy and what it means to be a consumer.

Today, we can look at the way that data integrates with ecommerce as a helpful component of a mission to make customers' lives easier, to make businesses run smoother, to tread more lightly and cover more ground. Ecommerce systems integrations allow us to move the dialogue from: What does data *reveal* about me? ...to... What can data *do* for me?

It's interesting because this perception shift is somewhat similar to how we want to revise our view of product, away from "What are this product's qualities?" ...to... "What are this product's benefits?" In both cases, **the way forward is to focus squarely upon data as the fuel for better experiences.** This is the purpose of integrated ecommerce - how can we weave together every possible system/resource/technique for solving the consumer's pain points more effectively? How can we employ "big data" in service of these positive goals, and solve better than the status quo?

LAWN MOWERS AND SUN HATS

Data is just another way of saying "information." The root Latin verb "informo" means "to form an idea," which I think is an interesting corollary here to ecommerce integrations. Data helps us *form an idea* of shoppers, of reasons for shopping, and of the effectiveness of shopping experience. **We form this idea simply by looking.**

Watch how the following data-driven observations lead to practical strategy, all revolving around the picture of the consumer which that data suggests: Let's say we sold 12 lawn mowers on Tuesday at an average price of $200. After adding a tracking pixel to a product page, we determined that many customers who browse lawn mowers also browse sun hats. By collating this data and cross-referencing it with Google Analytics tallies of conversions, we find that of those who complete a lawn mower purchase, 50% also buy sun hats. Our order management system tells us that overall orders of sun hats rise proportionately alongside lawn mower sales during the spring and summer but not in winter or fall. Our ERP tracks and predicts how many sun hats we need to order from our supplier to arrive in time for the next April's demands upon sun hat inventory. Our CRM identifies that customers in California buy double the sun hats of those from Oregon. Finally, our in-house "information warehouse" slices and dices group-edited spreadsheets to reveal that Facebook ads for lawn mowers which included copy referring to sun hats resulted in 30% sales increases for both products, but only when targeted to "home improvement" fans vs. "beach" fans, who did not buy any lawn mowers.

Now, you may have had a hunch before looking at any data that sun hats would sell well alongside lawn mowers, but now you have **detailed proof to justify your ad spend**, and a more honed understanding of how large numbers of customers prefer to shop and why. All of these insights are only possible with advanced systems integrations.

If we know that lawn mower customers are concerned with sun protection, a marketing team could then build campaigns specific to geography and season. Offering mower/hat bundles on the product pages and at checkout is a no-brainer. It might even be worthwhile to helpful to install a simple module on the lawn mower category page which integrates live weather data drawn from Google location services for each individual user. It's up to that business to decide how far to go with this integrated data, relative to what they understand about their customer. In every case, they can strive to offer **an improved solution** to a layered customer pain point which has been observed through data: "I need to mow my lawn, and the weather may require sun protection while I do it."

In this scenario, **we thought about the customer's needs, then applied the data we had in order to solve it, with custom integrations.** That's textbook great ecommerce. And it's human! We made the customer's experience better, and we sold a hat.

Data is the language.
Integration is the dialogue.

INTEGRATIONS ARE PARTNERSHIPS

Another great way to think of integrations is as "partnerships." Not necessarily with an individual or a company, but really, *partnerships with information.*

Why doesn't a *single* piece of software house, analyze, and act upon *all* data from *all* sources? That's a great question. It really comes down to the excellence of specialized tools for specialized tasks. Some tools can focus upon a very narrow field of information in granular detail. Then, a master concierge can pull only the bits that are relevant to given tasks, saving resources for where they're needed. Which tools you use to analyze any kind of data is a matter of preference, but what's important is that *the information itself* is partnered with the processes that need it.

Those partnerships can facilitate tasks. They can shed light on future conditions and prepare resources accordingly. They can collect and organize any business activity that can be measured. They can communicate that information from one person, provider, or process to another.

Integrating or partnering with information is inherent in all human activity. We glean input from one another, from our environment, from our bodies. As perceiving creatures, this dialogue is central to all life, and our businesses reflect that. **The more connected - *rooted* - a business is with other data-gathering systems outside of itself, the stronger its ability to provide value to every system outside of itself.** Hence the more reason it has to exist and endure.

REAL-TIME = RELEVANT

From a practical standpoint, integrations allow us to offer more "real-time" content, which is another way of saying more *relevant* content. Do you remember shopping in pre-digital retail stores and trying to find a size or spec that wasn't physically displayed in the showroom? The clerk would say, "I don't know, let me check in the back." Now, we've learned to expect instant status updates on just about everything - *where* it all is, *what* it's all doing, *when* it will rendezvous with me and my path. Every subject. Every product. There doesn't seem to be much time left for "the back" in the modern world, and certainly not in retail. Meaning, **information about the status of a thing has merged with the thing itself.** Think about that for a second.

A data feed which tells your order management system if there is enough inventory in stock to fill a customer request on the product page is an extension of that product. Its status and availability are just as important to that customer as its color and size. In order to communicate this important information instantly and seamlessly, unique connections must be in place between the systems that govern ecommerce shopping experience and the ones that monitor palettes in the warehouse.

For the consumer, more relevance throughout the shopping experience means a more *valuable* shopping experience. For the business: maximum awareness of any issue which may cause friction throughout the selling process, including delays, inventory shortfalls, etc. An automatically updating "Only 3 left!" badge on a product page is a great catalyst for purchase, but not just from a nigh pressure sales standpoint. If I really want that pair of sneakers in purple, I'd like to know how long I have until they sell out. **These integrations improve the shopping experience and reduces friction for both customer and business**. That's their purpose. That's the purpose of the technology - the only purpose.

"OFF-THE-SHELF" INTEGRATION?

When it comes to ecommerce data, systems integration is rarely as cut and dry as a single click, or "off-the-shelf." Nor would you want it to be. The reason for this is the unique complexity of each business' product, customer, and data. Mapping highly specialized activity data points to highly specialized software requires precision strategy derived from the business' special workflow - that's the art of it.

"Prepare an instant quote for wholesale accounts which calculates the current exchange rate in Canada and then offer a bulk discount of 17% for an additional 100 units from the customer's account wish list, as these items are currently in the overstock warehouse in Toronto" isn't exactly a button that ships with Shopify. But if this business knows that factors like country, exchange rate, wholesale pricing, local inventory levels, and pre-entered customer preferences frequently converge, it might be advantageous to devise a custom integration that taps external ERP, OMS, and CRM data to improve every customer's experience - and save worker's time.

"Hey, where's the widget that's coming in from Brazil and where's the one coming in from China, so I can assemble them both here in our plant, and then ship retail kits to Walmart before the holiday rush?" It's a mouthful just to say, let alone do. Before the advent of integrated ERP systems, we used to rely upon people to track these things, and when things went wrong, you either missed your deadlines, or your staff had to put in a Herculean overtime effort to hit their goals. The nature of a well-integrated series of systems is that you can consistently and reliably deliver on your commitments to your customers and your vendors, without often having to fall back to the man-hours that were *much* more commonplace in the analog age.

Obviously, every business wants a solution that is precisely dialed in to its exact modality and variables. Every business wants to get the most out of its partnerships, and not settle for "well I hope this generic answer happens to answer my question along with everyone else's."

Integrated ecommerce means "specific to my business." One-size-fits-all means "details don't really matter to us."

CHAPTER SIX

TRUST SYSTEMS

Somewhere in the last few years, "making the case for ecommerce" has given way to "making the case for ecommerce other than Amazon." This shift tends to obscure the larger picture of the global adoption of ecommerce, which is a tremendous victory-in-the-making for the way humankind does business, communicates, and lives. We have to remember that. Just 20 years ago, there were only about 300 million people using the internet at all. Today that number is closer to 4 billion, with annual ecommerce spending matched roughly a hundred dollars-per-user at 400 billion. The rapid shift toward digital commerce is part of a larger story of the "digitization" of humanity, a movement that still, despite these numbers, is in its infancy.

There is an enormous amount of ground yet to cover - and it might be helpful to think about this not in terms of how competitive one is against Amazon, but how effective a business is at furthering the macro-narrative of public trust in digital life. Why? Because we are on the team that thinks digital life is *improving* life.

The roadblock to this improvement isn't really technology or money. It's trust.

The question of trust is still at the heart of successful ecommerce on any platform, any channel. Trust in how effective a solution will be. Trust in the "word" of a company which is offering that solution. Amazon did not invent ecommerce - but it has clearly spurred and supported the spread of trust in digital life. This acceleration is a gift to all sellers.

How are you building a foundation of trust, with systems like transactions/payments, fulfilment/shipping, and cloud-hosted security? How is your shop advancing the greatest story of our time?

TRANSACTIONS AS TRUST

Just as the original ancient currencies required trust to be accepted as tradable stores of value, digital transactions must also have a strong foundation of trust in order to be viable. So, though our tools have changed drastically, we still rely upon trust in one another in order to thrive.

Customers who enter their credit card number to pay for goods on your site are trusting you with their money, their identity, their time. This is an act of good faith which is by and large mutual across countless thousands of ecommerce sites. Customers are trusting that you will hold up your end of the bargain, that if they pay you as agreed, you will indeed send them everything they've ordered. Payment *systems* - meaning, the service provider who uses customer-supplied information to move real money from one location to another - are conceptual manifestations of trust as much as they are practical services.

In the early days after the first major dotcom crash, many factors were coalescing which would create the perfect staging area for trust in a new form of trade. Broadband internet was taking hold around then, and nearly half of U.S. residents suddenly acquired round-the-clock internet access, as opposed to the cumbersome dial-up of years past. Investors had been given a strong whiff of internet commerce as a frontier of untapped market potential. The fallout from 2000's burst bubble was *more* serious investment in ecommerce, not less... "smart money" always buys in the red. To make that investment pay out, not only would new technologies be needed to support exponential leaps in scale, but there would have to be **widespread cultural acceptance of online transactions.**

Can you remember the very first thing you ever bought online? Full disclosure, my first online purchase was on Amazon. I bought an imported CD of Radiohead B-sides, something I could never find in my local record store, and for which I was apparently glad to pay $49.95! I was ecstatic. The current ubiquity of trusted online payment systems is so pervasive that it's hard to remember/believe that as recently as twenty years ago, paying online was still considered novel, and somewhat risky. But some of us found it very exciting.

Increasingly, we're seeing customers think of their payments as utterly invisible. That is not only due to familiarity, but also thanks to the increased sophistication of payment system integrations on ecommerce sites. Entering a card number at checkout usually does not inspire a crisis of trust these days - that goodwill has already been earned over and over via countless transactions, on countless sites big and small.

All consumers need to know now is if a brand is reputable, if security is assured, and if they can choose among various payment options that they are already well-familiar with. While the amount of funds transferred one way or the other will always be important, how it gets there is increasingly a non-issue.

Paying online with a credit card is a better solution than paying in person. Paying with one click is a better solution than entering a full credit card number. Simply waving a NFC device in the general direction of the transaction is even better. What will be next? We don't know yet, but we are all excited to get there. The only limit to incoming innovations in this space is the advancing trust of the consumer in each successive technique.

When I think about the questions that matter to customers around the subject of ecommerce payments, it starts to become very obvious that they *all* revolve around trust. It's interesting to think about **ecommerce platforms as technological guarantees of that trust.** The online transaction is an intangible thing - the customer and business are each in a sense *imagining* one another. The job of the platform is to create a total environment around this non-physical transaction which makes it absolutely trustworthy for both sides.

So how do you do that? Is it is simple as adding a security badge to a checkout page? Or leaning on a brand like PayPal or Apple to connote legitimacy? Sure. Those are tried and tested techniques. We *can* trust those brands and the technologies they have developed. But again, we want to look beyond the feature to the reason for the feature, as that is where we can protect the enduring trust of the customer. It's not "here's the latest doo-dad" - it's "it's in our interest and yours to foster an environment of safe transactions."

Whether offering a range of gateways and currencies, NFC terminals, mobile card readers, one-click, or one-touch, whatever... *everything should be oriented toward solving for trust,* and talked about accordingly.

NEW MOBILE PAYMENT PARADIGMS

Now at the close of the 2010s, most merchants can already get the benefit of a decade's worth of mobile payment innovations. When mobile internet usage first really started to take hold, the main payment-related issue for ecommerce customers was practical. No one wanted to go find a credit card, and type the number on a tiny physical keyboard and a very small screen. Today, this simple physical issue has been solved, by everything from enormous screen real estate, to simple auto-fill of forms, to NFC devices which process Apple Pay, to PayPal payments with the flick of a wrist. Most online merchants are already moving to secure most of these benefits for their customers.

The next paradigm shift in payments is clearly the social app, like Venmo, Square Cash App, and Apple Pay Cash, which are all rapidly becoming de facto ways of paying for things, from a consumer culture standpoint. Not that long ago, dividing the tab at the end of a meal involved a pile of credit cards - now, it's very common for friends to reimburse one another via Venmo. And since a broad swath of young people are keeping their Venmo money in their Venmo account, Venmo debit cards now allow them to use the platform as an alternative bank account.

Overall, merchants are positioned really well to benefit from the advance of these frictionless payments. They just need to stay mindful of the trends, and seriously consider any new app, device, or workflow which reduces friction around payments. That's always the question to ask around integrating these options - *how does it reduce friction?*

"Lack of trust" is a deadly form of friction.

CASHLESS BUSINESS

Is ecommerce heralding the end of cash? That may still be slightly aspirational thinking at this point, but a few key factors are definitely pointing in that direction. When I was a boy, I remember my father always keeping a certain amount of cash in the house. He was born in 1932, and reverberations of the various periods of economic hardship throughout the 1900s stayed with him and most of his generation.

For a long time we would hear of merchants who only took cash, and a public who would only spend cash. Well now, specifically in the time since the financial crisis of 2008, we see a new generation of young adults who have never experienced anything like a "bank run." They have widely used ecommerce for shopping since receiving their first credit cards, and have as a whole, fully embraced developing technologies. This is a perfect confluence of trust and lifestyle, which are symbiotically leading all of us away from using cash. Away from feeling like we *need* to.

The ubiquity of paying digitally has spread beyond the bounds of ecommerce - now we're increasingly in a situation where we expect as consumers that there'll be some kind of card reader or device-supported payment option at any kind of outlet that we spend money at.

Today, virtually everyone who works in a service occupation, from tow truck drivers to electricians, offers an option to pay by credit card, frequently with a Square reader or similar device attached to their phones. You can pay a parking meter with a debit card, buy a soda at the convenience store with Apple Pay, and then pick up a couple of tickets to a movie via the Fandango app, all without a dime of cash.

Ecommerce payments are so easy and so woven into how we live, that cash has now become a bit of a hassle to use, even when we leave the internet and interact with real vendors in

the physical world. This is indicative of a tremendous amount of belief in technology, and tremendous good will.

FULFILLMENT AS TRUST

Once the payment is made, the complementary system of fulfilment takes on the mantle of trust. Purchases gathered, packed, and trackably shipped are the basic expectation, and of course, fulfilment which executes exactly as described to the customer is essential for building trust.

There has been an interesting shift recently which really underscores this and throws it into a better context. Consumers, trained by a decade of ubiquitous free shipping from major retailers and Amazon Prime, have moved from "Shipping is a *premium* I have to pay to get my goods delivered" to "Shipping is a *right* I expect to receive in return for my purchase." This has inspired business owners to move from "Shipping is an *upsell* - a profit-driver which improves margins by adding to order totals" to "Free/cheap/easy shipping is an *incentive* which drives profit by leading to more completed purchases."

That's an important distinction. The former stance indicates a contentious or untrustworthy relationship between buyer and seller... i.e. the delivery of goods is emotionally uncertain, and must be guaranteed with money. Today, the seller demonstrates trustworthiness by assuming the burden of fulfilment on the customer's behalf.

Some online retailers still follow a model of using shipping fees to eke out a slight margin increase in the final moments of a transaction, as opposed to just passing on direct costs, or picking up the tab entirely. This can work to an extent, and the labor that is involved with preparing and shipping goods is definitely worth something. Your shipping department staff's time is worth money, packing materials cost money, and no UPS driver works for free. But hiked "flat" shipping rates to cover these costs is ultimately a bad hack, because it adds friction for the customer, is not personalized to the real costs of shipping each order, and lowers the solution value of the sellers' services. It is a violation of trust, however minor. **The whole point of ecommerce is to offer a less-hassle alternative to driving to a physical store.** Emotionally, high shipping charges are coming to feel like a "gotcha" to the customer, and this feeling is counter to the solution of any of the pain points they brought you.

TIME, DESIRE, AND EXPECTATIONS

By 2000, I'd made enough online credit card purchases to finally trust in the overall legitimacy of ecommerce transactions. Meaning, I wasn't fearful of the order not arriving at all, with the store owner already halfway to St. Croix on my dime.

Now, we've come to a point where confidence in speed of delivery and transaction security are both also relatively solved for consumers. As long as it's a reasonably functional and modern-looking website, most of us trust that the terms offered are relatively assured, delivery will be executed in keeping with promised timelines, and if not, there will be ample recourse to resolve any problems.

But back in the late 90s, that wasn't yet the case. In fact, in those early days, there were a lot of products and services out there designed to impart trust to the customer. "Hacker safe" and SSL seals were originally designed to solve the trust gap. The consumer was *perpetually* reassured about trustworthiness.

Today, our relationship with the fulfillment of orders has evolved. There's a lot of talk on the wind that people want same-day or Postmates-style, on-demand delivery. Much of this conversation is driven by theories that consumers now expect *all* deliveries in two days or less because of Amazon Prime. While I think those are decent heuristics to work from, there's more nuance to those expectations. The subtleties are not driven by technology or even habits, but by desire.

Let's say a new camera or some other premium electronics device came out and I'm anxious to get it. Then, 1-2 days shipping time is my expectation, because I have a strong and active desire to get that thing. If I'm ordering paper towels in bulk, I feel less urgency around the timing, and 4 days would most likely feel completely fair. In fact, like many people, I would probably forget I had even ordered paper towels and be pleasantly surprised by the time they arrived.

Our work then, as sellers, is to try to understand the motivations around customer purchases, and allow that to factor in to choices we make about fulfillment. The easiest way to assess desire is simply to ask, "when do you need this by?" A more advanced version of the question is "how often do you need this?" Consumers tell us, "I need it Tuesday," or "I need it every month."

So, if trust is established, and desire is assessed, you can start to form efficiency strategies which serve both, while maximizing your ability to retain margin. If, as a seller, I know that an order is expected on the 20th of the month and I can get it there for a small fraction of the shipping costs it would take to deliver on the 10th, I should optimize my fulfillment so that I ship on the 10th, pay very little money, deliver by the 20th, and everyone's happy.

This ability to **plan around expectations** is a key to the profitability of all fulfillment models, especially subscription sales. Dollar Shave Club doesn't have to take lower margin in order to rush delivery - it needs to spend as little as possible to deliver that razor on the first of the month.

THE THREE VITAL ASPECTS OF FULFILMENT

There are really three parts of fulfillment.

First, *where* do you have products distributed around the country?

In Amazon's case, sheer scale gives them an advantage for delivery that only a few other retailers will ever have. Amazon can store 100 copies of a Harry Potter book in 20 different distribution centers around the country, and when someone orders it, Amazon can accurately calculate that they can use a low cost book mailer from USPS and still get it there in two days, because everyone lives within 200 miles of one of those centers. Amazon can keep enough inventory on hand for popular products and have them spread strategically around the country to get things out quickly.

And then because of that, Amazon is able to use big data to very accurately predict their rate of sales for individual items. For those 100 copies of a Harry Potter book in 20 distribution centers, Amazon would have a fairly strong idea of how long it will take them to move them all.

We can learn from this, and either leverage Amazon's distribution network directly, or look at regional sales throughput and rent out our own regional storage warehouses.

The second piece of the fulfilment equation is the *speed* at which you can move things around the country. And while Amazon has had some impact on that, ship speed has really fallen upon UPS, FEDEX, and USPS to develop and execute. Amazon has certainly driven them, in the way a jockey drives a horse. This, combined with strong competition among carriers over 20 years of ecommerce, has led to mastery. Routes have been optimized, methods for combining ground and air transport have become infinitely flexible, and overall efficiency/options have increased. The cost to move a product across the country in two or three days has gone down dramatically in most cases.

The final piece of the puzzle is "the last mile," that final leg of the product journey from carrier to doorstep. Today, Amazon, Postmates, and other on-demand services are offering alternative methods for that last mile delivery. Independent retailers can employ some of these options, such as offering 2-hour delivery via Postmates for an upcharge, or again, they can simply lean on the big 3 carriers to sort out last mile logistics most efficiently.

SHIPPING AS SOLUTION

I've (unapologetically) had a Prime membership since 2005. That first year, I didn't see the offer of free expedited shipping as a threat to conventional retail, or the end of independent ecommerce sellers. I still don't. This development was a clear indicator that **a new plateau of trust had been reached between consumer, vendor, and the technological systems which bridged the two.** Here was a vote of confidence in favor of expanding the usefulness of ecommerce, and it was met with strong public approval for this latest "better solution." Amazon's investment in building an infrastructure of strategically placed warehouses, complex trafficking software, and robotics, coupled with swift and exponentially growing adoption, signaled that all parties had developed true trust in the culture of ecommerce.

Seen in this way, the competitive strain that Prime shipping exacts upon independent sellers is not "strong-arming." Is Prime essentially a marketing program disguised as a loyalty reward? Perhaps. But it's clear that customers are choosing the best possible solution to their problem. If a customer's need is "I want my purchases to arrive as quickly and cheaply as possible," then of course they'll choose the provider who can do that best.

Independent sellers are still charging too much and taking too long to ship goods. They are perhaps missing the bigger picture here - the key to increasing margins is not by increasing the price - it's by *solving the problem better*. The net result should not be a generation of sellers with unsustainably generous shipping offers. It should be a generation of sellers who demonstrably offer better solutions, period.

Like it or not, offering free and fast shipping is increasingly essential for all merchants. Within reason - we are not yet at the moment when large scale B2B customers expect a 2-ton palette to ship for free. But we're close. The business you gain from implementing easy, affordable shipping will outweigh the costs in the long run. And when it comes to living with Amazon, **expensive, slow, and cumbersome shipping will be the death of your business.** This is the developing answer to a long-running consumer pain point that we are collectively solving.

At every decision, ask, how is this new solution building trust? Do real-time calculators add transparency to product pricing? Do a wealth of options for speed and carrier add a degree of consumer control to "flat" rates? Do branded carriers let us piggyback on the trust those brands have already earned? Do automated tracking updates alleviate fears of lost packages? Do online/brick and mortar pick-up combos demonstrate that a custom solution is your top priority? Do free shipping offers over set order thresholds acknowledge the value of a customer's business and build a dialogue of mutual respect?

These kinds of questions position you as a *peer* of Amazon's, not an inferior. You have a common goal.

If UPS tells you that they have a huge hub in Fallon, Nevada, you might want to build your fulfillment centers there. With that little bit of strategic thinking, almost any online retailer today can leverage the expectations that have been set by the market and by Amazon, to offer a similar - and equally valuable - experience.

CLOUD ECOMMERCE AS TRUST

The concept of cloud computing is central to complete ecommerce, and is the vessel through which all of our trust systems travel. The whole idea of highly-integrated complete ecommerce depends upon it, with all of the data required to power every activity we've discussed hanging at-the-ready for instant non-physical deployment to any relevant system. It's a wild concept.

Ironically, many people who use the cloud for storing, transmitting, or accessing data don't have a strong grasp of what it is - **adapting to new non-physical paradigms is a process which takes time to unfold and embrace.**

Most consumers don't realize that even the software which runs a business no longer "lives" at the site of the business. Yet, the fact that cloud-based Software as a Service, or "SaaS," ecommerce platforms are as stable and secure as they are has certainly been a key to why we trust virtually every website we see.

Cloud computing uses the internet to deliver every key computing service there is. From remote servers, users of the cloud (which really, is just another way of saying "data on the internet") can be served everything from storage space and bandwidth to the elaborate software systems which support their businesses. Here's why we like it: it is the easiest way for your business to store, repair, backup, upgrade, and scale every piece of data, all customer information, all transaction information, all web content, as well as the ecommerce platform it sits on. The cloud is the ultimate bottomless well of information, protection, and process, and *all* of it exists to protect the dual interests of customer and business.

With good cloud-hosting, you typically don't have to share any performance features with other users. At any time that you wish to scale up (or down) computing resources like storage or processing power, it's really as simple as one click. If hardware needs to be repaired or replaced, you don't have to experience any downtime. Cloud-hosted data can be redundantly backed up over an array of servers, which protects your data in case of catastrophic failures or delays due to upgrades.

The more nimble all of these resources are, the more they can respond swiftly and accurately to the demands of business and customer. That is the purpose of cloud computing: **make the allocation of resources more streamlined, affordable, and responsive than physical infrastructure.** Complete ecommerce strives to balance fine control with automated management of the actual server environments, for maximum cost reduction - and pain relief.

HIDDEN DANGERS OF CLOUD ECOMMERCE

The non-physical nature of cloud computing does open sellers up to some very particular hazards. Older laws and conventions of business were built around physical operations, and though we are moving away from this centralized model, new customs don't materialize overnight, and there are some actors who will use the lag to their advantage.

For example, merchants in other trading nations such as China can build an ecommerce site with a dotcom address. Everything about the site can appear to be a U.S.-based company. These merchants can sell products online and ship them directly from China to consumers in America. Because of an obscure policy within the postal service which discounts the shipping of low cost items internationally, overseas sellers actually have a significantly unfair advantage over U.S. sellers. So, the overseas merchant can currently ship products like cheap jewelry, generic appliances, and knockoff apparel all the way to customers in the United States for less than it would cost someone in United States with those same products just to ship it within the United States.

The point here isn't to rail for or against protectionism, it's to show how **cloud ecommerce and modern ecommerce design have obscured distinctions of country, quality, and ship speed**, to the point where consumers may suffer with inferior service.

Laws and cultural customs will be sorted out over time, to reflect the new cloud reality. But the takeaway for now is, if you're not thinking about leveraging the freedom of the cloud to improve efficiency, you risk being targeted by those who are.

But here's the good news: the efficiency gains of cloud ecommerce are so significant, overhead is so low, margins so high, that the potential to scale into a much larger, more successful company is suddenly far more plausible.

Cloud-hosted solutions dramatically increase convenience, but they do open up sellers to forms of attack that wouldn't be an issue in a 100% physical business. The notoriety of high profile data breaches in the 2010s has been relentless and inescapable. It's in the air and on the minds of customers more and more. Just the generalized *fear* of insecure personal data can erode trust, even if there is no attack.

One of the more famous site crashes in history was suffered by the fashion retailer Bonobos, whose site was down for almost a week, starting on Black Friday 2011. The problem was due to a massive amount of traffic and orders slamming into a fundamental architecture problem in Magento, the business' ecommerce platform.

It was the worst possible scenario. The website was up, and customers were placing orders. But while the Bonobos site was collecting the money, the orders weren't logging, so the site was getting floods of money with no way to tie it to customer accounts. Imagine if you think you just gave Bonobos $200 for two pairs of pants, and they got your $200, but they do they do not know anything about which pants you want, who you are, what your address is, or how to contact you. Now imagine how likely you'd be to shop with that business again. Imagine how likely you'd be to shop with such a business after simply *reading a news article* about the crash.

If customers lose faith in your ability to protect their data, funds, transactions, and your ability to deliver goods, the value of your brand and product lowers... ergo your ability to command the margins you need to survive also lowers. So, all sellers need to invest in security, and then need to communicate to everyone that this is always a top priority.

In the highly competitive environment of modern ecommerce, we want to avoid giving customers *any* reason to leave our sites. Even with no attack, basic site downtime can have the same trust-killing effect. I recently heard a downtime horror story from a large-scale enterprise business which been the target of a brutal DDos attack in the middle of the night. While their data was not directly compromised, their site was down for several hours, and their ecommerce provider at the time did not have dedicated customer service available at 3am. As it turned out, a large share of this business' traffic was in international time zones, resulting in a loss of daytime business of more than 100k. The full costs of the downtime were incalculable, because it's impossible to say how much trust was lost that day.

Do merchants and consumers need to live as if one of these hypothetical tsunamis is definitely going to be coming one day or another in the near future? Unfortunately, yes.

So, the enhanced efficiency of cloud services must be balanced with proper investment in redundant backups, timely security patches, and mechanisms for transparency in the face of trouble. Trying to pass off a cyber attack as "site maintenance" is a poor choice, because remember, we are always looking to establish trust with these services. Lying does not serve this goal. Customers will trust your brand more if it is forthcoming and to the point.

TYING IT ALL TOGETHER

Okay, so you've selected an ecommerce platform that can be customized to you and your customer's needs. You've explored the features which can be used to make the case for the value of your products and services. You've integrated with data systems that add value, improve efficiency, and reduce friction. You've built trust by understanding the essential problem-solving value of payments and fulfilment. You've reduced costs and protected your data by hosting in the cloud.

Essentially, you have begun to use the "master's tools." This toolkit is your ticket to staying protected and competitive, by offering your community the best possible solutions, the best possible experience, and the earned trust that will sustain your venture for years to come. Now, you're ready to leave the nest.

PLATFORM CHEAT-SHEET

FLEXIBILITY

Can comprehensive features, workflows, and site experience be customized without breaking the store?

EASE OF USE

How steep is the learning curve for basic daily admin?

FEATURE SET

What are the native feature sets for custom design, inventory and order management, and merchandising?

SPEED

What are average page load speeds?

SECURITY

Is this solution backed up with failsafe protection?

CREATIVITY & CONTENT

Is there a CMS which makes content easy to work with?

RESPONSIVENESS

Will my store be optimized for mobile and all devices?

EXTERNAL SELLING

Can I manage externally hosted products from my control panel?

PAYMENTS

Which payment gateways are supported?

CUSTOMER SERVICE

Can I create self-service customer service tools for orders/returns?

INTEGRATION

Can we "play nice" with other systems like an ERP or MailChimp?

REAL-TIME VISIBILITY

Is live data about orders, inventory, shipping status, etc. pushed through instantly to all relevant systems?

HOSTING

Is a secure hosting plan included and easily adjusted to conditions?

SCALABILITY

Are there limits to the amount of products, pages, or traffic?

IMPLEMENTATION

What is the average time to design, build, troubleshoot, and deploy a total solution?

COST

How are licensing fees, monthly costs, and upgrades calculated?

TEAM

Who will I be working with directly and how accessible are they?

AGENCY

Will I be able to contract out design, development, and advertising to external agencies?

COMMUNITY

Is there a strong and active customer following?

PART III: CHANNEL

Is it better to specialize or go broad? Is it better to cast the widest net, or to become the master of a very small kingdom?

The question of "where to sell" is vexing - because **the channels you choose to sell in directly define what solutions you are offering.** "Should I sell my goods to wholesalers?" is less of a strategic debate and more of an *identity crisis*. The venues and devices you use to sell your products are intertwined with the definition of those products. So how do you choose to develop one channel's shopping experience vs. another's? And do you have to choose?

It's interesting to examine "omni-channel" as one of the trendiest ecommerce buzzwords of this decade. The word did not gain popular usage in an ecommerce context until about 2010 - this is according to Google Trends, which failed to register any search data for the word since such rankings began in 2004, and now ranks it as having achieved "peak interest." Retail ecommerce platforms all tout *the omni-channel strategy*, essentially implying "be all things to all people." This constitutes a real bucking of the previous era's largely B2C-oriented emphasis.

Now, efficiency software has enabled leaner teams to run far more complex shops, leaving extra resource bandwidth for branching out. A pet food manufacturer can sell treats online and also at a point-of-sale popup at the dog park. A game designer can sell in-app purchases, and also run a premium subscription blog which explains how to use them. An athletic wear distributor can add different custom branding for different resellers, to be sold on independent sporting goods websites, via apparel-specific marketplaces, and in high-quantity wholesale orders for local schools. Omni-channel, in marketing-speak, has come to mean "untapped opportunity" - ingenious re-pairings of product, customer, and venue.

Not only can modern ecommerce software equip you to be a specialist in a broad range of channels, it might actually empower you to redefine what a channel is, and can be. I'd like to explore the ways in which our definitions of discrete channels are evolving, or just maybe, *dissolving altogether*.

CHAPTER SEVEN

ONE BUSINESS, MANY CHANNELS

A NEW DEFINITION OF CHANNEL

Imagine you are a manufacturer of home improvement goods - tools, electrical gear, fixtures and décor. You have a brand name which has accumulated consumer trust and good will over time, primarily due the exposure your products receive on the shelves of big box physical retailers like Home Depot and Orchard Supply Hardware. You've recently built an ecommerce website to offer more customer-direct B2C sales, and have loaded the site with great content and resources. You also maintain a brand page on Amazon featuring a selection of the same products, which you ship from your own warehouse using Seller Fulfilled Prime. From customer feedback, traffic analytics, distributor conversations, and sales results, you gain some interesting insight: your shoppers are shopping in a very unusual manner. Customers walk the aisles of Home Depot holding your mobile app in their hands, scrolling through the exhaustive product content and reviews that you have posted, which they use as live research when looking at those products on the physical shelves. At the end of this process, some customers complete their purchase in the store, some add your items to the cart on your website, and some navigate to Amazon to complete the purchase there and ship by Prime.

The question is: *which channel are you selling through here?* The customer for this kind of product needs a lot of information - technical specs, how-to-guides, social feedback, with more depth and complexity than can be found on a basic Amazon product listing. They also like to touch and handle the products, but would like the benefit of a full selection from a manufacturer rather than what's locally in stock. Finally, some would rather let Amazon deliver it to their door than have to load it in the car themselves. These customers have straddled digital & physical storefronts, shopped from both a retailer and a manufacturer, browsed product content from at least three sources, used a mobile device, and gave their business to an online marketplace due to convenience, which actually sent the order to the brand's own warehouse. By cobbling together various venues and techniques, **the customer essentially created their own channel.** How, as a seller, do you specifically support this kind of business, this kind of a "bespoke" sales channel?

We used to use the word "discrete" when defining channels, i.e. one distinct and separate class of audience, with one distinct method of communicating/buying. Usually, channel consciousness applied to wholesale vs. retail, and whichever channel you chose dictated starkly different business practices. It seems now though that the hard and fast lines between channels are not as accurate or thorough as they once were.

Channel-specific selling is predicated on a few assumptions: first, that audiences with common goals will tend to shop in the same way. Next, "channel" assumes that established historical trends of those audiences can used to predict future behavior. Finally, channel assumes that there is a single "voice" which speaks effectively to this group as a whole - voice meaning mode of selling, way of addressing priorities, way of satisfying needs.

The problem with these assumptions is that they don't reflect the paradigm shift that has occurred over the past decade, largely since the mass adoption of smartphones - upwards of 2.5 billion users on Earth and 75%+ of American adults as of 2019. Obviously this level of all-day access to internet content has impacted the adoption of ecommerce, but on a deeper level, it's interesting to look at how this movement has prompted a sort of *identity mobility*.

Case in point: I am a lifelong hip hop fan. I love everything about this genre, and have informally studied it for decades. I had impressive collections of vinyl hip hop records in the 80s, hip hop CDs in the 90s, and hip hop mp3s in the 00s. Then a funny thing happened. Along with my Pandora and Spotify accounts, I acquired many new "favorite genres." It turns out I also am a fanboy for indie pop, modern psychedelic rock, and a good amount of EDM when the mood strikes me. My record collections are largely hypothetical now, and take the form of hundreds of unique playlists crossing genres and eras to create my own unique personal DJ set. The upshot is, I am much more well-versed in many more forms of music than I used to be - and I think of myself as a "hip hop guy" much less.

Just as music streaming services have largely obliterated the need to wall off different genres of music, in favor of massive random access to all music all the time, so too are shoppers more likely to cobble together an individual grab bag of sources, opinion, and options from countless providers, modes, and traditions. It's just how we live right now. So, planning for expansion into new sales channels is tricky. It's not entirely clear who will be there when you arrive. It's less helpful now to strategize around, "what channels do I need to invest in to expand my business and number of customers," rather than to simply ask, *"where are the people whom I want to sell to?"* This is a subtle yet powerful foundational adjustment, and a beautifully inclusive **new definition for channel.**

Today, "channel" is another way of saying "where the customer is."

Part of orienting to the customer solution means dropping stereotypes and presumptions about how "everyone" shops. There is no "everyone" anymore. Every customer is now the author of their own personal sales channel. So, the big challenge for all types of sellers going forward is not diversification of resources, but **building approaches which are open-ended and overlapping enough to accommodate increas-**

ing diversity.

A rigidity of approach here will lead some sellers to find new hurdles in reaching the retail customer. In the most basic practices, some elements of B2C retail ecommerce have scarcely evolved since the late 90s. The essential building blocks of even the most sophisticated modern ecommerce sites, such as a database of products, a product page, a shopping cart, a checkout page, were all already in place at the very beginning of ecommerce. For all of the advances between then and now, we still represent and sell products in this exact same way.

However, the way people prefer to shop has evolved *dramatically* in that time, with occasional massive paradigm shifts. **If we look at minimal viable retail ecommerce as the first major paradigm, the second would be the rise of mobile, and perhaps the third the dominance of marketplaces.** As the bulk of sellers adapt to each paradigm shift by upgrading features, accessibility, marketing, integrations and the like, those who are more “disruptor”-oriented are already asking the question, what will be the next shift? What comes *after* Amazon, and how can I lay a foundation for that future, now?

EVOLVING CLASSIC SALES CHANNELS

In discussions of classic channel divides like physical vs. digital, desktop vs. mobile, even expert vs. amateur, we increasingly see less of an "either/or" mentality, and more of a "yes, and." Less rooting in a single approach, such as dumping 100% of resources into brick & mortar, or removing 100% of resources from brick & mortar, in favor more freedom and cross-channel experiences that are seamless to the shopper. A combo like "Order online and pickup in store" may not be the dominant solution for most consumers, but the concept is leaning in the right direction, because it acknowledges that **individuality in the shopping experience** is what's becoming the norm. However each industry, business, or customer wants to define it... "mix & match" being the surprisingly simple perspective shift. In other words, *it is mattering less and less which channel the customer prefers.*

An interesting effect of the past two decades of internet culture has been **the blurring of the lines between casual audience, fan, and expert, and a growing unity of professional and consumer audiences.** Expert-level granular knowledge of any topic is always one Google search away. DIY content and selling platforms, plus endless online discussion of every topic have shifted the mantle of authority away from companies and onto individuals. Nerd “superfan” communities stopped being outsiders a long time ago and now constitute the mainstream of American life (see: box office receipts for all Marvel films). Appreciation of any brand or product is a common denominator among all levels of fans, clients, experts, or providers - harmonizing with that *appreciation* is the key for transcending the lines between “first in line at ComicCon,” “Netflix subscriber who likes superhero movies,” and "national retailer who stocks Iron Man action figures." Is there a way to speak with all of them at once?

Their interests are what create the channel, not the venue. We can apply this thinking to all types of selling.

What I'm getting at here is a direct brand-to-customer modality which is less tethered to any one conventional outlet, or conventional approach to selling to an individual market. Highly customized ecommerce solutions are the way to express this in reality.

B2B AND THE DAWN OF MEGA-CHANNEL

According to Forbes, B2B ecommerce sales are projected to top 7 trillion dollars worldwide by 2020, more than double that of B2C. Because of this staggering growth, the B2B ecommerce channel that has been especially responsive to changes in physical and digital culture over the past 5 - 10 years. We can surmise that this is perhaps due to the volume these sellers work at, which accelerates the need for *innovation at scale.* For example, high volume B2B sellers need to store more goods, more efficiently. This leads to investment in digital warehouse managements systems which make scanning easier, the development of applied robotics in those warehouses to increase efficiency, which in general makes warehousing costs go down. This in turn allows sellers to add warehouses in strategic locations, then orchestrating their activity from increasingly sophisticated digital control systems, which lowers operating costs, reduces drag on fulfilment, and supports higher sales volume.

These types of developments are fostering a strong growth environment for the B2B channel, but interestingly, they are also addressing new preferences for how people actually like to sell and shop, which transcend traditional seller/buyer roles.

Historically, the term "business-to-business" has meant "I'm selling some sort of part at wholesale to people who use them to assemble a new product." For example, let's say I'm selling ball bearings, and then those ball bearings get turned into remote control car wheels, they get turned into ceiling fans, all sorts of things. They become a component of a bigger product. Today, the concept of B2B has grown broader than that. Really, **B2B is about selling a product, good, or service that simply enables another business to *do something*.** It enables them to either offer their own product, or build their product, or package their product. It's purpose-oriented. And digital systems automations are opening more avenues for more people to sustainably pull off more of this purpose. So, what must a seller do to take advantage of these new opportunities?

Hands down, the key issue for ecommerce merchants addressing B2B sales is this: **People expect a consumer-level experience, oriented to a professional-level reality**. Collectively, we are no longer open to accepting a limited or subpar experience when ordering something for a business, versus the slick experience we get when ordering something for ourselves personally. At the end of the 2010s and beyond, all online experiences now have to be "slick."

Given the need for bespoke B2B-specific buying paths built into the ecommerce experience, plus the new tendency of all shoppers to expect a "slick" experience, how can we orient this channel to provide the best of both worlds?

Another question you might start to ask about B2B is, *why is it important that we differentiate whether this is a business that sells to other businesses or business that sells to consumers?*

In the world of ecommerce, this distinction is important simply from a feature set standpoint - the tools you need to sell to businesses, such as volume pricing, unique discounting on a per-business basis, unique payment and tax terms on a per-business basis, etc., are not features that are used at the retail level, and are not universally available in ecommerce software.

So yes there's a distinction in knowing if a platform can serve very specific functions which B2B customers tend to want. But on a deeper philosophical level, the answer is no, it's less important to sort clients into wholesale or retail piles than it used to be. All products are simply "things people buy" - whether they're buying it for their business or themselves is becoming less and less relevant.

The only reason you care is from a strategy perspective. So if I was selling ball bearings and I know that in general they get bought by the 100-pack, I shouldn't go out of my way to list them as single items. Sales and marketing strategy are impacted as well, as who you're talking to is always a factor in deciding what to say. But ultimately, do I, as a hypothetical business owner, care? No. And that's because **channel-specific buying habits are expanding to overlap and encompass one another.** Everyone, I mean everyone, wants a fast, relevant, beautiful and modern ride.

B2B and B2C are merging into one multi-faceted channel.

It seems like there are two converging paths represented by this merger – total *personalization* (ultra-relevant shopping experience and content for customers), and at the same time, total *customization* (best practice structures for the unique workflows of individual businesses).

As a business' ability to customize its ecommerce operation grows, more customers will gain access to increasingly personalized experiences. That's the dynamic. It's not just in B2B/B2C, it's everywhere - within micro retail communities and macro channel concepts like mobile-first selling. The channel, however it's defined, becomes more about finding the sweet spot between the need of customer and business, than about rigidly setting all techniques to benefit either consumer or industrial shoppers, mobile app shoppers or conventional desktop browser shoppers, eBay shoppers or Etsy shoppers, etc.

I'm recommending this approach to clients because it stands to reason that our definition of "omni-channel" in the eras that will follow Amazon will open into something more like **mega-channel** - elaborately hybridized approaches to highly personalized customer needs.

In fact, *mega-channel* might mean the dissolving of old existing barriers between any particular type of business and any particular type of customer. It's a form of economic evolution that collectively we are only barely beginning to grasp as possible. This means more opportunity for more customers and business to find more specialized solutions. And that's better for everyone than a binary choice of A or B.

DE FACTO WHOLESALERS

Here's an interesting question, given this dissolving of roles, why shouldn't all businesses become full-time wholesalers of their own products and use Amazon to handle 100% of retail sales? Is this the direction of retail at least, and if so, is this concept more cost effective than investing in building an independent ecommerce site which serves both B2C and B2B? The truth is, not all businesses and products could possibly support this model sustainably. Here's why.

First, products that are exclusively sold on Amazon are hard to protect. As we've already discussed extensively, by "protect," I mean *establish unique and exclusive value which no other manufacturer can match*. Especially if that other manufacturer is Amazon itself. There is a bit of an urban legend in ecommerce that Amazon studies sales figures for neo-commodity products, and then replicates production for any top sellers that can be copied. A simple product search for common household items from appliances to athletic socks will bear this "legend" out.

A great example of the tenuous nature of protecting products against Amazon is Monster Cable, a manufacturer who for years sold very high-priced stereo and computer cabling. The cables themselves were commonly available cheaper from many other companies, but Monster added aggressive marketing/branding around their version of the product to justify pricing. In time, Amazon reproduced identical generic versions of many of these cables under their "AmazonBasics" banner, at a price that was at least 10x lower than Monster's. As a consumer searching for "HDMI Cable" on Amazon, you'll be shown Monster's version at $119, and AmazonBasics' version at 3 for $6.99. Which option will the majority of shoppers select?

If the product is easily duplicated and there's nothing inherently proprietary in it that you own or possess, Amazon (or another manufacturer selling there) can replicate the product and just cut you out of the process altogether. Which makes sense for Amazon. As the original seller, we then have to consider if the 50% cut we'll be giving to Amazon right now to host and fulfill our products is worth the reduced sales we'll eventually see as a direct result of this soft poaching. You (constantly) have to define and protect the unique value prop of what you offer. So, eliminating the Amazon platform from your repertoire altogether may be a way to shield against this phenomena. However, if Amazon doesn't knock it off, someone else may.

Beyond that, the reasons against placing all retail business on Amazon are largely mathematical.

Even if you have a more unique product that is selling at a lower volume, Amazon's still going to take half. That's just the general rule of thumb. So if you have a product that will sell on your website for $100, you'd have to sell it to Amazon for $50. So let's say you're able to manufacture it and get it to Amazon for a total production cost of $30, which means you'd make $20 every time a unit is sold via Amazon, vs. $70 for every sale on your own site.

The math equation is, will the increased exposure you get from Amazon selling/promoting your products result in a net gain of traffic and conversions on your site which outweighs the $50 you're "losing" on each sale? Are you able to move units at a far greater volume on Amazon than you could on your own site? Or at the most basic level, do you want the exposure you generate within Amazon to stay within Amazon? If you don't have an independent retail site at all, consumers who discover you via Amazon will only interact with your products there. If you offer an option - shop thru Amazon, or shop on your boutique site, at least *some* of the search and social activity your Amazon listing generates will lead users to your site, where they may make a purchase. This is, for now, the best of all worlds.

INDIVIDUAL APPROACHES TO CHANNEL

There are plenty of business-to-business products that have no real need to ever be placed before a business-to-consumer audience. So the question then becomes, is it possible to sell to multiple distinct audiences at once, and moreover, is it necessary?

Each business needs to do an analysis on its unique product, as opposed to saying, "you really have to be able to sell at a convention and you have to be able to sell to wholesale customers and you have to have a retail site and you have to have marketplace presence."

To the extent that there is such a thing as "have to" when it comes to omni- or mega-channel, we have to remember that these concepts can mean very different things to different businesses. So if I'm selling diesel engine blocks, omni-channel could mean that I just need to have inventory in three locations with inventory control, so that my dealers can know how long it's going to take to get from the warehouse in Nebraska versus the warehouse in Louisiana. That could be a type of omni-channel. If I'm selling athletic socks, omni-channel might mean dividing my resources between direct sales on my website and wholesale sales to specialty brick and mortar running stores.

Ultimately, the idea of an ever-present buying experience across *every* conceivable venue is not going to be true for every business. That's why I discourage cookie-cutter *anything*. So, a balance must be struck between open-minded, open-ended concepts of channel, and understanding your customer so well that you don't waste time over-extending where you don't need to. That's today's tightrope.

CHAPTER EIGHT

LEARNING FROM MARKETPLACES

The interesting thing about classifying what a marketplace actually *is*, is that it can fit into *many* categories - yes it is a platform, yes it is an ecommerce website. It is a banker, a marketer, a community of peers. It is a company, but also a brand. It is a commercial experience, but also a social experience. These all-inclusive descriptors really reflect the direction that ecommerce as a whole has moved and grown.

The point here is that your business is all of these things too. The barriers between such distinct roles are becoming less entrenched. Conversely, the many roles any business is expected to fill are growing.

Is it better to wall off distinct audiences and use different machinery for each, or to build an approach that goes beyond "omni" to that "mega" place, wherein anyone who interacts with us can find a home, with solutions specific to them?

Innovation comes from looking at the existing structures and adding to them. To the extent that we can remain less in "battle mode" and more open to the ideas the dragons deliver, juggernauts like mega-marketplaces will point the way to what we ourselves can achieve - and better. That's the perspective shift.

THE SOCIAL MARKETPLACE

Historically, the marketplace was as much a social gathering place as a base for commerce. In ancient Greece, an "agora" was a blend of trading stalls and political rallies. The 3000 shops of the 17th century Grand Bazaar in Turkey functioned more like a self-contained *city* of resident workers and shoppers than like a retail center. Even the massive Mall of America in Minnesota draws as many people for its theme park rides as for its tenant stores. This tendency for the blending of channels and mixing commerce with social culture is inherent in the marketplace concept, whether it's called a mall or a bazaar... or Amazon.

What we see with Amazon is an ancient concept that has been swept up in and modernized by the larger digitization of all facets of human life. Looked at in this way, **the social solution that Amazon offers is just as important as the shopping solution.** If we want to learn how to use or compete with this phenomenon, it's helpful to look beyond price, fulfilment, navigation, etc., and ask how Amazon tries to deliver solutions which at once feel *very personal* and *very universal.*

Why is the virtual bazaar so resonant with sellers and shoppers? Not because it has the best selection of items, or the best price, or ships the fastest, but because consumers have been trained to accept this "place" as supporting *whichever* of those facets is most important to them. The strength of a marketplace platform lies in its ability to reach and serve specific customers, within a specific class of products, but using ecommerce tools to offer multiple groups of totally disparate, specifically-focused solutions simultaneously.

This is perhaps the most generous definition of the marketplace channel of all: *a place where you'll find what you're looking for*. This should be an aspirational goal for all ecommerce sellers. The following is a big picture game plan for how to use these dragons to get there.

HACKING THE BEST AND WORST OF MAJOR MARKETPLACES

As we browse today's key marketplaces, it's interesting to look at them in terms of what customer need is being addressed (solutions that we can build upon), and next, what are the existing friction points that hold each marketplace back (friction which we can interpret and solve for better)?

Here's the hack: in what way, however big or small, can you *directly* address the key strength and weakness of each of these marketplaces?

Amazon answers customers' need for convenient and comprehensive access to nearly every (retail) product category that exists on Earth. It has solved for distribution/fulfilment like no retailer in history, yet. And it has leveraged the power of its brand to become synonymous with these solutions in the mind of the customer, practically to the point of being a basic utility in the world of ecommerce. So here we see three solutions to emulate, in the most general sense: connecting customers with answers, connecting digital product discovery with physical satisfaction, and wielding brand to make the case for both. In what ways is your business prioritizing these *same* three things? If your answer is something like "I'm offering my product as a honed-in solution to the common customer problem I have identified, I have implemented free or expedited shipping to get those products in hand more easily, and the signature of my brand is to point out the value of those two solutions," you're on the right track. **We can protect the business against Amazon by essentially neutralizing the uniqueness of its three-pillared pitch.**

We can apply the same kind of concept to any of Amazon's chief flaws, as we understand them today. Despite its breakthroughs, Amazon continues to lack the degree of personalization that will need to grow only more specific as time passes. Product discovery remains highly simplistic and generalized. Customers are herded after-the-fact by observed behaviors, instead of anticipated through intuition of their real-life needs. So how do we use this insight? How do we "weaponize" it? If your answer is, "Aha! The more personalized my ecommerce presentation is to my specific customers, the more I am able to fill the void into which Amazon has dropped the ball!" - bingo!

This is how to capitalize on the "missing scales" you identify in any of these dragons, and then to throw your spear in that precise direction. Take the focus away from fearing how much market share they've gained in your segment. **Put the focus on prioritizing plans which are informed by their strengths and weaknesses.** Dragons are instructive in this way, they are guides. If Amazon's largest friction is poor product discovery pathways on its site, how can you innovate more creative and effective ways to discover your own products on your own site?

It doesn't stop at Amazon. You can use this same kind of conceptual approach with any dragon. eBay, for example, is to a degree founded on hyper-personalization. In many ways, it allows vendors and buyers to negotiate and set their own terms for transactions. This is its greatest strength. So again, as an independent seller, how can you apply a note of that winning solution to what you do? Is there a way to offer more personalized pricing or terms for your customers? It might come in the form of something as simple as "VIP discounts," or as elaborate or price groups for high-volume corporate clients with unique credit terms, etc. The point is that we analyzed why eBay is succeeding at a particular solution, and then took that as inspiration to use on our own business, at our own scale.

We might see eBay's fatal flaw as the lingering stress around high-pressure auction-style transactions and limited "whatever fell off the truck this week" selection. Okay, so now we can solve for those issues on our own scale, perhaps by designing a user-facing shopping experience which is intentionally not stressful, ditching the old fashioned "act now or else" mentality and steering customers toward the value of fully-concierged, high-end boutique shopping. A limited selection can be presented as "curated and elite" as opposed to "limited time only." These are just suggestions, but you get the idea.

Google Shopping is the most integrated with organic search (a powerful solution), and also the least user-friendly shopping experience of all marketplaces (a powerful flaw). So, separate from the question of whether or not to promote products there directly, we can step back and take some conceptual cues for how to "protect" against this marketplace. A: put some love into organically cracking the SEO code so that your independent site is increasingly visible to customers launching a product journey on Google, and B: invest in a storefront that's ten times as creative, informative, and interactive than Google Shopping.

Finally, if you're feeling adventurous, we can look to the massive success *and* massive shortcomings of Alibaba. Thanks to cheap international production, Alibaba is able to host a large amount of B2B-oriented component parts and goods that can be re-branded by resellers, with volume pricing. This makes Alibaba a valuable solution for B2B buyers looking for economical sourcing.

But, along with that cheap pricing comes questionable quality. The lack of known brand name manufacturers further erodes the perception of value for customers. And as the majority of items ship from overseas, U.S. customers are in a for a long wait, for goods that are frequently not even manufactured until *after* a group of orders is placed.

To piggyback on Alibaba's best solution, try incorporating high volume price breaks to B2B customers without them having to import from overseas on their own. And if one of Alibaba's weaknesses is that users interpret products not being manufactured until after they are ordered as a potential quality issue and an inconvenience, perhaps you can present the concept of a "pre-sale" as a feature not a bug for exclusive-hungry shoppers.

And so on and so on. Every single marketplace, no matter the size, has inherent solutions and limitations which point the way to innovations even the smallest home businesses can address relative to their own operations. **This is not fighting the dragon, but riding it.**

That's why I recommend studying these dragons from a place of appreciation. **Appreciate what works and appreciate what doesn't.** These are direct guides for which parts of our own businesses to develop. It's an enormous strategic gift.

MARKETPLACE TAKEAWAY

I think overall we are seeing that by offering a range of sellers, extreme choice, and membership in social communities of buyers, marketplaces challenge conventional ideas of channel and encourage approaches which are diversified at the top and specialized at the bottom.

Just as with all other parts of the process, if a marketplace builds on/adds to the value you provide around your product, it serves your brand and product. Whether or not you use its services. Better yet, make it plain to the customer that you have considered, matched, and improved upon every convenience they think they'll be getting through any marketplace. That's game, set, and match.

8 WAYS TO APPROACH NEW CHANNELS

01 INDUSTRY

Which segments within your industry are currently under-serving customers?

02 BRAND

Can you elevate "distributor" into "taste-maker," highlighting your role in selecting, negotiating, and fulfilling products?

03 SHOPPING EXPERIENCE

What are the inherent obstacles/requirements for say, a home tablet shopper vs. point-of-sale at a trade show?

04 EXCLUSIVITY

Are there exclusive qualities, such as branded or short-run products, which can be offered to unique groups of customers?

05 PRICE

Can you create logic-driven rules to offer personalized pricing (volume/subscription/etc.) for a range of accounts?

06 AVAILABILITY & ACCESS

With relevance top of mind, can you offer custom workflows, highly curated presentations, and real-time content?

07 SPEED

How do factors like region and use-case dictate the speed of fulfillment you can and must provide?

08 CUSTOMER SERVICE

What data do you need to wrangle in order to reduce demand on reps and equip them with channel-specific answers?

CHAPTER NINE

SCALE AND TRANSITIONS

Is the targeting of a new market the way to grow your company? Today, we can scale, in a sense, simply by increasing the size and breadth of our audience. In a world saturated with social media advertising, we can really reach a titanic audience overnight. We can scale our resources by adding storage and bandwidth with one click. And by integrating with our partners, we are more prepared to share the workload of doing omni-channel business than ever before. So why not start selling to *every* conceivable audience, right now, today?

The common theme between "scaling" and omni-channel expansion is this: the foundational elements of our businesses *must* be sound before the outreach can begin. Before we can grow "out," we have to grow "up." Before we can add revenue in new channels, we have to build a strong and sustainable basis.

Can you create a non-commodified product? Can you display that product on an ecommerce website, supported by content that makes the case for its value? Can you provide the services, innovation, and reputation which justify the margins you seek? Can you fulfill the promise you've made, and get your goods into your consumers' hands as the pinnacle of a customized, personalized shopping experience? Can you apply technology to reduce all friction around that shopping experience, around every single place a customer interacts with your brand?

Then and only then can you ask, "Can this idea be profitable, effective, sustainable in an all-new channel? And if so, what new channels can I sell to? What new problems are there for me to solve?"

What a wonderful launching point for growth: ***What new problems can you solve?*** That's not just the character of scale, that's the *reason* for scale. Any discussion of omni-channel selling or scaling must originate with this motivation - the drive to solve more, better, in new places, for new faces. The breakdown of old channel distinctions is serving us - the more nuanced and flexible a channel is, the better it will be able to inspire the right solution.

I've worked with many examples of businesses that have very strong multichannel sales operations which they run from one ecommerce platform. Your business might successfully juggle a trifecta of direct sales website for high margin sales, listing on Amazon to compete directly with other sellers while driving traffic/awareness, and eBay for overstock items. This is a great template for scaling by channel.

The exact answer however will be different for every kind of seller, depending upon where they are along the spectrum of size, complexity, and reach. The thing about scaling is that it's never "done," you never fully "get there." Ideally, you'll *always* be striving up from where you are, wherever that is.

VIABLE DIY AND SMB

The first hurdle for any kind of scaling is always going to be *viability*. For a **DIY** business that sells a single or simple product line from a very small home base, the goal posts are still that sustainable minimum viable business model.

Usually this is a one-person operation, as in a sole proprietor, and they typically are going to have a very simple website that's moving as little as one order per month. So we're talking about something incredibly small. The vast majority of Shopify or WooCommerce businesses fall under this category. These two platforms combined have about 1.2 million storefronts out there, and of those, it would be a safe estimate that as many as a million of them fall into this DIY group.

That's around 85 percent of sellers which, if they got just *one order per month*, would be satisfied.

I have to say that there's something very inspiring and even romantic in the businesses these people are trying to create. The magic of the entrepreneurial spirit is what drew so many of us into this field. But it's still more like a hobby at this level in the sense that, these sellers are still trying to figure out if there's a market for their product *at all*. A very low amount of money is put into inventory, perhaps only at the scale of hundreds of dollars. The costs for operating and maintaining the website are probably also low, let's say less than $500/year. The seller probably accepts Square or PayPal only, in some combination which reduces or eliminates monthly fees for payment processing. If they have 20 orders in a year, they feel successful - and relative to their goals and scale, they should.

"SMB," or small and medium business, would be firms that are doing less than a million dollars per year in online sales. There are a lot of viable companies that are processing much more than 20 orders per year, but still not quite breaking that million. Those companies also tend to have a sole proprietor who's running shop, with a small staff for logistics, IT, customer service, fulfilment/warehouse, accounting, and marketing. The head of the company is really making any critical decisions, and then they're outsourcing everything else, whatever doesn't require any specialized knowledge about that particular business.

We might say that difference between DIY and SMB is viability. An SMB is an actual business that someone is earning some or all of their income from, whereas no one in the DIY space from what I'm describing is actually living off of that income. There are certainly a substantial number of DIY sellers who want intensely to become a true SMB, but they may not know how to get there, or perhaps their product line simply doesn't support the inherent demand needed to scale. This feeling of *reaching to the next plateau* is the romantic part. A lot of people in the DIY space have aspirations for their "hobby" to become their full-time job. SMB has achieved this marker, and is looking ahead to the next leap.

THE LEAP TO "COMPLEX" OPERATIONS

For a **"complex retailer"** or enterprise-level seller, vast product catalogs and highly complex operations generate business with very large and established audiences. At this tier, orchestrating the movement of an elaborate supply chain is required to offer the most sophisticated "hybridized" shopping experiences possible, bridging physical and digital stores, a range of devices, and highly personalized UI options, in order to offer customers the ability to fine tune their own interactions with the brand.

Here, the opening of a new channel can indeed become the gateway to greater scale. One of our more inspiring Miva clients is Lotus Sculpture, which has a primarily B2C business based upon selling fine art at the consumer retail level. This company imports the most gorgeous, larger-than-life statues, carvings, and other artifacts from Asia and India - a product which is so unique, so hard to source, and so physically unusual that it might seem impossible to run a high-volume ecommerce business around it, let alone scale up to the complex enterprise level. Well, while there may be an inherent upper limit on the size of the original retail audience, new audiences could be developed in completely different channels, in this case B2B. For example, the company may decide to offer its artwork on a large scale to hotel chains and offices, addressing corporate buyers. In this way, new channels are an excellent way for businesses to contemplate growth.

There are many different ways to go from SMB and mid-market "complex" sales, all **incorporating the expertise you've learned around a product line when operations were smaller**, because a lot of the tasks at hand are still the same. You're still shipping products, still hiring a bookkeeper to handle your accounting. The decision these business have to make is, *am I selling the right mix of products? Do I want to keep expanding on this line of products? Do I want to open a totally separate business? Am I selling on the right marketplaces*? And then you get into advertising and brand exposure... *am I leveraging the latest in social media? Am I leveraging the latest ad buys?* Those are just some of the challenges a business faces.

The leap an SMB must make to achieve mid-market status is

just as profound as the leap from DIY was. Honestly, these same kind of leaps happen at *every* stage of growth. And I don't care how big or particularly successful you are, those leaps are never easy. Technically, financially, socially, or emotionally.

I would even assert that our first trillion dollar companies in the world, Apple and Amazon, will have to go through *massive* growing pains if they are to become two or three trillion dollar companies. Things just don't scale forever as they are. But for smaller businesses, right as they're hitting that million dollar mark, they tend to come into a sort of *existential* question.

You get to a point with these businesses where they start to run bigger numbers... "If I'm selling a thousand items a year at a thousand dollar price point, how many more items do I need to sell to get from one million in revenue to two?" One problem is that there may not actually be enough additional people willing to spend a thousand dollars on your product. So the seller may have to sell, say 3000 items at $700 to get there. It depends upon what your clientele is and how broad the addressable market is, but oftentimes for businesses to go to the next level of size, they have to adjust a core tenet of their existing business, and that can add a lot of complexity. This kind of moment is generally known as a **"time of transition"** and it's very common for all businesses. At these times, all are hoping to ultimately get the massive benefits of scale, but the transitions can be perilous.

You basically have this viability test over and over again, and as you hit each new plateau, you'll have to prove your viability again.

ON THE WORD "ENTERPRISE"

At Miva, we use **"enterprise"** to describe any business bringing in more than a million dollars per year in sales. In conventional commerce, the word is often used to describe more than 100 million dollars in sales, with everything between 1 and 100 referred to as "mid-market." But our use of the terminology is more generous because *our industry is young.* In the world of ecommerce, there are *only* approximately 50,000 stores in North America that are doing more than a million a year in sales. This is a very young market, relative to conventional commerce.

When Miva debuted, we were one of the first ten or so ecommerce platforms that ever existed which one could buy. We were initially oriented to the traditional definition of small business, though from a technology standpoint, our product wasn't very different from the straight-up "enterprise" tools of the day. The unique skillsets of our team led organically to selling what was essentially the first mass-market SMB ecommerce platform. As our ambitions expanded, so did our lexicon. Companies like Miva, Magento, Shopify, and BigCommerce have all started to mature, from an age perspective, and I think we all have started using the term "enterprise" as an aspiration point for all smaller businesses. As it should be.

The democratizing effect of online media - essentially, everyone has access to everything - means that for a shopper, the scale of any one business' operations is not that relevant. It is only relevant if it leads to a better solution for that customer. A shopper who needs a new pair of shoes will buy from whoever reaches them with the best argument, whether that seller hand-makes boots in a workshop, or is a distributor of thousands of other types of apparel. So, all retailers regardless of size end up focused on the same thing, which is **"What does the customer need, where are they shopping, and can I serve them effectively from my current size and business model?"**

SCALING IN A DIGITAL AGE

Many of the core principles of scaling are not new concepts, and obviously they pre-date digital. Building awareness for what you're selling, then beefing up your ability to produce and distribute to the new people that you're showing it to you.... that's not new. But there are key differences today which point to new ways of growing physical operations and channel-oriented outreach which are unique to two factors: our tools being digital, combined with the mobile revolution.

Successful scale always boils down to an *inventory* challenge, a *marketing* challenge, and a *deploying-to-market* challenge.

Most successful growing businesses are masters of one of these three. An importer of international art pieces would specialize in procuring inventory, and build a business model around that. An apparel reseller might specialize in marketing via social media, and use mastery of Facebook ad content and targeting to be the centerpiece of the business. An auto parts seller might have an outstanding marketplace pipeline, leveraging Amazon listings within a very specialized product segment.

Adding digital tools to each of these specialties - inventory, marketing, and marketplaces, brings the ability to add scale dramatically faster than in previous eras.

For example, if you were trying to scale marketing in the seventies, decisions would have to move through layers of bureaucracy, including an ad agency, account reps, designers, department managers, producers, traffic supervisors, etc. The machinery of all this is inherently more expensive, cumbersome, and slow. Whereas today, if you want to coordinate and deploy ad buys for your company, any company, you can do it the moment the creative is done, with a team as small as one "jack-of-all-trades" owner who is also the creative director, etc. A Facebook campaign which reaches targeted audiences with millions of members can be conceived, produced, budgeted, deployed, and seen by the public in a matter of hours or less.

Digital gains in the realm of inventory procurement have also been profound. The ability get products sourced, manufactured, and delivered in a very short time now has perfectly aligned and scaled with global consumerism from the seventies forward.

"Marketplace management" is a new term for the internet age, but before we had Amazon and eBay, we still had the concept of sales channels in previous decades. If you were selling to, say, Target, Sears, or Kmart, you typically worked with individual buyer reps who specialized in those companies' specific practices. A lot of time was spent going to the offices of these reps and shmoozing - that's how you got a distribution deal. Now, there's no shmoozing. What used to be a game of relationships to get through one of a handful of distribution channels is now a self-service model that's just straight up *pay-to-play*.

The amount of freedom that modern sellers have to "turn up the gas" so easily does come with some downsides and dangers. Certainly someone who knew how to play the political game at a Walmart or Kmart or some other large distribution channel could carve out a better deal for their company. Because those dynamics weren't being purely driven on purely ROI data like Amazon is, personal influence and salesmanship could affect your ability to get higher margins.

Whereas today, the essentially mathematical basis of Amazon, with humans barely even involved, means that **unless you control the product, unless you have something unique about your ability to offer this product, there's no margin left for you.** You'll be stuck in the middle of game being controlled by an algorithm set to optimize sales of toasters, not of *your* toasters. The pay-to-play model of the marketplaces has really made it so that average margin goes to Amazon, it goes to the house.

We also have to consider how quality of work life and non-work life is affected by the speed of advancing scaling technologies. A prominent ERP platform recently started calling itself a "business management platform," and the sales hook is the ability to have every piece of information about your business right there on your phone. It sounds tempting at first, until you realize that this constant data overload means you're working 20 hours a day. **"More effort" is not what really drives scale. It's about leveraging less work, more efficiently, to grow sustainably.** A 20-hour workday is not sustainable.

REALISTIC EXPECTATIONS (REVERSE ENGINEERING THE ALLEY-OOP)

The time it takes to scale to different revenue plateaus is going to vary wildly by product. Tesla selling a $100,000 Model S is going to have radically different growth complexities than someone selling a $10 battery charger. The numbers are relative to both the business and the profit potential. Tesla scaling to a million dollars in sales effectively meant that they'd sold 10 Model S's. Meanwhile, selling a million dollars in battery chargers at $10/each requires selling 100,000 units. So, the revenue plateaus are going to be different by product line. Those plateaus come with management complexity.

No matter the complexity, any business working towards growth needs to be an expert in at least one of the 3 pillars we identified which support scale: **inventory procurement, marketplace management, or advertising.** Yes, you can bring in consultants to direct these activities, but the more high level strategy you farm out, the more of your margin goes into the bank accounts of your consultants.

The more successful you get, the more complex these pillars are to wrangle. Essentially, there's a point at which you're the only one who knows how to do something right and you realize you can't do it all by yourself anymore. So this is the first plateau, regardless of the dollars that go with it. You get to a point where you can't grow the business any farther because you're literally putting 100 percent of your available cycles into doing the things *only you know how to do*. The process of teaching and training others to do what you do is frequently like having to let go of one side of the mountain just to grab the other.

So let's say you get to a place where you're taking home $100,000 a year in income from your business, and you now realize, hey, I need to hire and train an operations manager who's going to handle my inventory procurement and getting my products shipped. I'll have to pay them at least $50,000 a year, and I'll have to train them and build a system in which they can best operate. This diverts my time and resources such that not only am I paying out what used to be half of my income in salary, I'm also not free to do the work which was earning me $100,000 in the first place. As a business owner, I don't know how to pay my mortgage and live that way.

This basic math problem is essentially what's waiting for all businesses at the precipice of each new scale plateau, and it always comes up, in one way or another. You are the little boy with his fingers in the dykes trying to keep the water from coming through, and at some point the water is going to overpower you. And the only way to actually fix the dyke is to pull your hands out, let the water flow through the dyke and then patch the dyke properly. Those things happen when you scale out of the ability to operate as a 1 or 2 person team. Then you have another set of issues when you get past a 6 - 10 person team. I would say most of the people we see in the world of ecommerce get stuck at that second jump, with few making it to the next jump up to 20 - 30 employees.

A great mentor of mine once explained this to me as a sports metaphor. The first level of mastery is similar to how golf is played - with one athlete, perhaps a coach, and a caddy for support. There is a very small management architecture in this, because largely the principal doesn't need a lot of management. The golfer, the coach, and the caddy all know the sport and don't need to highly organize their strategy around common tasks like, how to line up a putt.

Even Tiger Woods doesn't have a standard operating procedure for how to line up for a putt. His coach doesn't write down, "this is the Tiger Woods method for lining up for a putt" and then hand him a slip of paper before he steps onto the green. There's no product marketing manager running around filling out an excel spreadsheet about how Tiger lines up for a putt. He just knows how to do it. That's comparable to how a 1 - 2 person business operates.

As you graduate to 3 - 6 employees, the business must necessarily acquire management layers, and starts to operate more like, say, a volleyball team. Think about how any sporting team of more than two, less than six people playing simultaneously must coordinate their plans and efforts with one another. At this level, you most likely have pre-set plays, whether it's "bump that spike," or an alley-oop in basketball. Point being, there's a coach with a playbook, and there's a methodology for practicing those plays. The goal is for all of the players to be able, through rote memory, to perform all the pieces of the puzzle that they're going to be required to do. No one's thinking when they're running down the court, "Oh, I wonder what the process is for the alley-oop." Through practice and training, you've cultivated reflexive actions that you follow in the moment.

And I think that applies very directly to business. When you're a 6-

person company, you have the leader of the company who's making the decisions about what to sell and what to charge, with master expertise in one of the three areas we discussed. Then you're going to have an accountant. You might have an operations person who's making sure that the packages get out the door, and you probably have two or three customer service people. In a company of that size, the leader of the company is certainly capable of doing all six of those jobs - if the bookkeeper quits, the owner can get into QuickBooks and make sure the bills get paid. If their customer service reps have the flu, the owner can handle a customer service call.

As these numbers keep scaling up though, the peaks get harder to manage alone. At 30 - 50 employees, the leader of the company can no longer do all of the roles. Now you're more like the head coach of a pro football team. You have a solid understanding of what your special teams coach is teaching, but you probably are not capable of stepping in to train your team if that person doesn't come to work. And so there's a point at which the leader of the company can no longer do all the roles and they're simply not capable under any circumstances. They're capable of having an opinion. They're capable of shaping priorities, of allocating resources from the larger view. And so, what rock-solid systems have been built to manage and sub-manage the growing array of tasks and challenges that leader's employees now face? And are *those* systems viable, sustainable, profitable?

A DRAGON LEADS THE WAY

Here is a tough pill to swallow for all sellers - the economy will continue to function just fine with or without your business. Amazon will go right on selling without you. But as an industry leader grows, everything in that industry stands to grow as well. Call it the "halo effect." The number of people shopping on Amazon and triggering all of their related services and ecosystems is not just growing Amazon's revenue, it's growing the entire ecommerce economy, and creating new channels that didn't exist just a few years ago.

Let's be honest, though: a consumer doesn't think about "channel."

They are simply solving their own pain points. They are driven by a practical concern - "My gas cap broke!" or an emotional drive - "I'd look great in that bathing suit!" They have a need, and you have a solution to that need, which they found via any number of access points. Whether it's a referral, a website, a pop-up shop, doesn't really matter. **In all channels, customers want convenience and maximum pain relief.** To this end, they will continue to define their own channel - their own pathway - derived from the myriad individual choices and options which serve them.

Every account is its own channel.
Every device is its own channel.
Every zip code is its own channel.
Every customer is their own channel.

This is the only defensible position going forward. Nothing less than the utter customization of all ecommerce, rising fluidly to meet the infinite configurations of consumer desire. When choosing where to sell, the question is moving from "which channel" to "what if?" What if my customer wanted to do *this*? How can I help them get there? What is standing in their way?

This includes Amazon but is not limited to it. The collective investment of humanity in ecommerce ultimately supports *every* business which sells online, plus partners like shippers, payment gateways, and analytic software, etc.. This moment is building a stronger basis for *all* to do business, in countless other forums. **That's the interesting duality of an industry dragon - for all of the opportunity it crowds out, it also creates opportunity on a greater scale than ever before.**

As Amazon scales, so do we all. This is an important point - and a very bullish POV. There are so many subtle ways in which a robust ecommerce economy inspires the continued growth of its many components and many channels. The question is, how will you carve out a space in this massive surge of abundance - a tidal wave really - sweeping through every conceivable channel you could ever sell in?

PART IV: CUSTOMER

The first time I was a part of a professional sales team, I was only 23.

I was hungry and ambitious, but didn't yet know all that much about adult life, and had only a starter perspective on the world of business. But this hardly matters to 23-year-olds. They just kind of charge forward blindly into challenges, and I was no different. I'll never forget picking up the phone to make that very first pitch to a prospective client. I had already been training for six months before I was put on my first solo call. Even though I was by then fully versed in the company's mission, and could recite all the bullet points, nothing could really prepare me for the rush of emotions which surrounded talking to an actual customer. *Will I know what to say? Will I come off as even remotely knowledgeable? Will I make a sale? Will I make a fool of myself? Can I get out of it? No, I got this... I could make a killing!*

By the end of that call, I learned a powerful lesson about interacting with customers, one which still informs a lot of my thinking today. You see, I'd been so overwhelmed with the tangle of emotions about my performance - how *I* would do, how *I* would appear, that I missed the whole point of the call - to listen to what *the customer* had to say. What issues were they bringing to the table? How well of a fit was my solution to their problems? And if there were blank spaces among all those bullet points, areas in my pitch that failed to address what the customer needed, how might I use the assets at hand to fill them? These questions were the real basis for the conversation the customer wanted to have. While my confidence - and anxiety - were drivers for me to give a high-energy talk and make a sale, to the customer my emotions were irrelevant. To the customer, anything other than the exact solution they needed was noise.

These days, a lot of the clients I speak with are not at the entry-level of ecommerce. They are usually seasoned pros who already run high-volume enterprise sites, and need to explore much more complex analyses, but the core dialogue always comes down to, *how can we use all of this technology we've amassed to make our business run better and make our lives run easier?* It's the same question which their customer is asking them. So when I say **the customer is the true driver of all ecommerce**, I mean we are in the business of being *helpful*. Our customers need to find ways to apply the great advances of modern technology to their own lives. We can meet their problems with answers, and meet their anxiety with hope - *this is the job of everyone who sells.* We don't have to *capture* them, or predict their every move - we just have to *listen.* To the extent that you can embrace this, and let it guide your decisions concerning all facets of your business, will you find more success on those nerve-wracking sales calls, and every other place you and your customer meet one another.

CHAPTER TEN

PERSONAS & PAIN POINTS

THE ULTIMATE MVP - YOUR CUSTOMER

Our evolving ideas about the product, the platform, and the channel partly come from observation, partly from experience and training. But the real reason these things move and change over time is because collectively, **customers are *always* asking for something better, a new way, an easier way, *more*.** Ultimately all of those other elements have developed in order to better answer the customer's question, which is always in motion, and always ready for the next improvement. This is a good thing. It's almost like you are relieved of having to *invent* topics for your business to explore, you are relieved of having to lead the discussion, in a sense, because the customer is always the one leading it. Ecommerce businesses are generally not charities - they exist to make profits for all of the people working for them and with them. But the way this is done is by **solving customer pain.** It is the customer's desire - and dollars - which inform every decision in ecommerce. Without their "direction," all of our decisions are arbitrary at worst, educated guesses at best.

If you want to see why a business, any business, is successful, you will always find that **they have cracked the code of their customer.** Who is this mysterious character? What do they need? What's missing from their life experience and how can I help them get it? How can I speak to them in a language which they understand? How do I stop trying to *control* their behavior, and instead learn how to *align* with it?

Yet, surprisingly few ecommerce businesses are approaching their shops from this point of view. It's understandable. Just getting that box onto the truck safely and on time, paying your staff and keeping the lights on, sometimes feels like a daily miracle. There's not a ton of time to stand in front of a whiteboard arguing with your social media manager about who your buyer personas are. You're in the middle of a *war*. But the thing is, taking the time to realign your focus to those questions of what the customer wants and how they talk about it is your *liberation* from that war. Because you're not in a war with Walmart, or Amazon, or your vendors, or your competition down the block. You're not in a war with anybody. You're in a dialogue, with one person only.

Stop trying to *control* your customer's behavior. *Align* with what they are already doing. Help get them to where they are *already* asking to go.

WHERE THE ECOMMERCE CUSTOMER BEGAN

The original ecommerce shoppers really had to be dragged kicking and screaming onto the internet. The benchmark of the first 10 million live websites took nearly 10 years (plus all of the preceding history of humanity) to achieve. Today there are 1.5 billion+ websites. Let that astonishing figure sink in for a moment. And in an important sense, we're just getting started. From 2016 to 2017, the total number of websites *doubled*. We are in the bend of a exponential curve. The *rate of growth itself* is growing.

If we look at ecommerce's portion of the total U.S. retail sales figures across the same 10-year time period, we see growth from 0% to nearly 10%. What do I think when I see "10% of all retail sales"? That's easy. I see 90% left to go.

None of this expansion is just happening randomly. Google didn't just wake up one morning, decide to invest a trillion or two into publishing websites, set their magic elves about coding it all and then just delivered the whole platter fully realized to America. In a grander sense, Google barely had anything to do with it. **It is the collective interest, engagement, and investment of the people of the world which is driving this relentless expansion.**

We needed a method of shopping that was easier and more efficient than driving to a store. We needed access to all of the many innovations of companies around the globe. We needed an affordable way to improve the quality of our lives, by picking and choosing from enough specialized options that we could satisfy our every daily need with precision. We wanted to have more fun while we shopped - we felt an innate need to be dazzled with sights and sounds, words and ideas. We wanted to find new and better ways to connect to other people, to form communities and share opinions, to find new platforms to shout from. Some of us just wanted a platform from which to troll. All of us - individuals and businesses alike - wanted to enjoy the very best consumer experience that our hard-earned dollars could grant us.

Ecommerce was an answer to all of these things.

A couple hundred years ago, this continent's economy was based on *trading beads*, a practice which continued well into the 1800s. Today, the U.S. GDP is at 20 trillion dollars per quarter. The point here is to zoom out and show the tremendous leap forward, from bartering with shells and stones to the modern complete ecommerce experience, and to show that it happened *fast*. On a historical scale, it is possible that we have just entered the first bend of the technology life-cycle S-curve, perhaps still hovering with the "early adopters." There is so much expansion yet to come.

We have no idea how long the current conditions will last, but we can say with certainty that the way we do business will continue to evolve very rapidly. The “unbeatable” dragons of today will be the jumping off point for all new innovations tomorrow. What won’t change are the fundamentals of the *customer* - desire and demand, resources and access. As long as you serve and solve for that customer, you will be able to do business no matter what the shopping trends of the day are. This is the key to dealing with fear over the potential migration of customers to Amazon. Customers won’t be “stopping” there - they will *always* move to the next, best solution to their problems.

Businesses that survive will be the ones which use emerging technologies to continue to solve for the customer’s problems effectively. Beads or bitcoin, this advice will never fail you. You protect them, and your relationship with them, by serving them *better*.

WHAT DOES THE CUSTOMER WANT?

In "The Hitchhiker’s Guide to the Galaxy," Douglas Adams invented a creature called the Babel Fish, an actual fish which, when inserted in the ear, could translate any language into the wearer’s native tongue. A universal translator that whispers the meaning of what anyone says is a tantalizing concept. Wouldn’t it be great, as a seller, to get a direct translation of everything the customer is trying to ask for, in a form which you understood and could act upon? This is really the thinking behind the modern ecommerce platform. With all of the product content out there, with all of the different channels through which people shop, with all of the third party providers who add various supporting ingredients into the stew, you need some kind of *central hub* which not only manages it all, but makes *sense* of it all. Most importantly, the role of the ecommerce platform is to facilitate clear communication back and forth between customer and business. Not just DMs to customer service, but *all* communication. All decisions, all sales, all clicks, *everything*.

In time, we can use our interactions with many customers on our sites to build portraits of their lives, honing in on why they shop the way they do, and what solutions they are looking for. Before they even get to a specific product journey, they are each motivated by emotion, by a need. Ecommerce requires us to deduce these needs.

Define the customer by *what they want.*

Before they have even found your ecommerce site, perhaps before they have tried your products or heard of your brand, it's helpful to think about the roots of your customer's quest. How does the public feel *before* they've met you, and how will these feelings give rise to more concrete preferences and needs? We need to know this in order to begin to assess how well we are capable of delivering on those needs, and more specifically if we can deliver on them in a better way than the customer's current solution, or lack thereof.

Basic human emotion is always the opening statement in a customer's relationship with a product and brand. They are expressing this emotion to you. Of course, real world customers will rarely have their needs defined in a single clear-cut category, and will instead hew together an amalgam of emotions which describe their priorities as correctly as possible. Some won't exactly know what their own emotional states are, not in words. By imagining the question, *"what do you want?"* we can help coax out a clearer problem, or "pain point" to solve.

THE PAIN POINT

We have looked at customers' desires as the launching point of their total shopping experience. From there, it's helpful to now think about how those desires manifest as "pain" in the customer's life. I put that in quotes because we are not usually talking about literal physical pain. In an ecommerce context, pain is simply a problem - another good basis for defining those customers, because it frames their desires in the form of a specific puzzle which can be solved. **The more specific the problem, the more dialed-in the solution can be.**

"I want to feel happy" is a lot more ambiguous than "The poor audio quality of this particular pair of Bluetooth earbuds is making me unhappy." The latter is relatively easy to solve, while the former could take a lifetime to unravel. Can we offer someone deep, true happiness by buying a product, any product? That's probably a more nuanced debate than we have time for in a 200-page book. But we absolutely can make their day easier, more enjoyable, and more productive with that product. We just need to know the pivot points upon which those positive emotions hinge for that specific person. So, when exploring what drives our customers, it's instructive to get as *specific* as possible.

Specific **customer "want" fuels a solvable "pain point."**

Customers in the grip of a pain point are in a state of dis-ease. We really want to know the exact cause - was it a bad experience with a previous product? Are they feeling some new form of unhappiness that was brought on by a recent change of conditions? Has internet content influenced them into an opinion? Do they think of their problems as just "the way it is" or "the way it's always been"?

Trying to understand customers turns you into a detective. You need to assemble clues and then interpret them. If the customer says, "I'm not safe," it's hard to help them. If they say "My car does not have airbags, and that makes me feel unsafe," we can sell them a car with airbags. So, keep zeroing in.

If we think our customer cares about wellness, we need to know how the last protein powder they tried agreed with their stomach. If they are motivated by quality, we'd like to know that they think generic tissues are not as soft as the name brand. If they seem frugal and driven to get the best deal, finding out that quality cameras are priced too high for them is invaluable information. And so on.

They key to building up a true portrait of your customer is starting with an emotional context, and then looking for natural ways in which that context grew and was expressed. Then we can take a customer who is interested in browsing sofas, and add the understanding that they think that comfortable products are worth a premium(general), and then that their current sofa is painful to sit on (more specific), and then that they have found shopping for sofas online more difficult than visiting a physical showroom (even more specific.) Even if we broaden out those insights to an entire class of customers, we've still got a pretty well-defined pain point: "Buying high quality sofas online is hard for many people because they can't assess the quality of materials from a picture." Doesn't this immediately suggest some potential solutions? Many more than if we only knew, "customers like quality." Our solution gets more precise because it originates with the customer's distress over *current solutions which aren't satisfying their emotional needs.*

BUYER PERSONAS

Can we break down all customers into generic "types" which can then be marketed to with automatic funnels? In a rudimentary way, this is how Amazon groups its customers - are you the kind of person who clicks on sneakers frequently? Are you in the group that has purchased a particular sneaker? Have you ever clicked on the "athletic footwear" product category? Well if so, congratulations, you're now in a specialized segment which will be shown more pictures of sneakers, more pictures of the sneaker you already bought, and sale announcements any time there's a site-wide discount on high tops.

But this is hardly an intuitive understanding of that customer. It's entirely "after-the-fact," and this is the main flaw in a click-based analysis. For to truly understand buyer personas, we need to look at **what conditions in customers' experience are causing them to shop for your product.** This *root* view of your customers is far more valuable than knowing exactly what they purchased yesterday (although we'd like to know that too).

Let's say you bought a pair of Nikes, but you did so because you're an avid runner, training for a marathon, who needs professional-level medial support and does not want to pay boutique retail process for it.

Next door, your neighbor bought the same pair of shoes, though they rarely exercise and only made the purchase after seeing Justin Bieber wear an identical pair on Instagram.

Same purchase, same product - but should we approach both of these customers with all the same tools, offers, communications, and everything else that goes into shopping experience? The customers are solving for very different problems - one needs quality and health, the other needs relevance and cool-factor. If we show each of them the same pair of sneakers without personalizing the presentation in any way, these two shoppers will not be able to understand why this shoe is uniquely perfect for marathon running, or why this shoe is uniquely popular and trendy. *If we don't know why they are shopping, we don't know how to sell.*

The more general your understanding of your customer is, the less accurate your sales presentation will be.

That's why if we invest in discovering core customer motivations (problems) at the start of our selling process, we can better shape the shopping experience we offer to directly address the unique pain point of that customer with more relevance and greater chance for success.

Shopper 1 might be saying, "I can't find a running shoe which meets all the technical requirements of training for marathons." Shopper 2's problem is, "My current sneakers are out of fashion."

Those specific pain points will make a great basis for a successful sales campaign. We could now go one step further, and assume that similar pain points are shared by larger groups of people. There are probably a lot of "people who need great training shoes for running marathons." There are also probably a lot of "people who want to wear the same shoes as celebrities." So we could say that just by identifying specific pain points, we've identified two distinct **buyer personas** for this shoe. It's a great exercise.

The risk for all ecommerce sellers and platforms, including Amazon, is that these two shoppers, who both ended up buying the same shoe on the same day, might get identical shopping experiences... They will both see the same set of upsell products at checkout. They will both receive the same automated marketing emails featuring that shoe and other shoes like it. They will both be offered the exact same incentives to buy more shoes. They will both be given the same terms/options for payment and delivery. Generic solutions may work, but are not as effective as they could be. The customer, herded into categories of other shoppers who don't have the same pain points, has no real reason to shop here again - and as a result, their loyalty may go to Nike and not to you, the seller of this pair of Nikes.

How do we transcend the inherent limitations of formats which must be at least somewhat standardized? How do we see past the generic insights that click-history provide, and get at a more complex, human understanding of the people we sell to? How do we bridge the distance between what we imagine or want our customer to be, vs. the somewhat less tidy reality of what they actually *are*? How does their reality harmonize with our brand, and how does it diverge? These are important challenges.

Ignoring buyer personas and simply adding more variations of what's already selling is putting the cart before the horse. That's really all that a recommendation engine like Amazon's is doing when it suggests products. You know what that says to the consumer? "Here's more of the same." **The status quo is rarely a strong solution to a problem.** It's better to ask *why* - "why do you feel the way that you do?" - and start to personalize the total shopping experience around that.

Customer voice is the question. Brand voice is the answer.

Speaking to this "persona" directly is paramount. This priority is compounded by the somewhat harsh fact that most customers do not really care *where* they complete a sale. Quite simply, the customer is looking for convenience. They want to know that they're getting the best price from whatever options they have. They want to feel that their time is well spent. They want their problem solved. What they don't do is organize their shopping habits in the way that ecommerce marketers do. No customer launches Chrome and thinks, "I'm going to enter this site's sales funnel and be led by the nose to the product this company wants me to buy." Whether they are shopping for themselves or their business, **they are launching a product journey from need and emotion**, always.

That's why I say that product discovery is awful on a site like Amazon. Yes, you can show everyone who bought a pair of Nikes more pairs of Nikes ad infinitum. But the customer's identity and specific needs are ignored with this approach, which makes the experience less successful for *everyone*.

As sellers, we can't possibly be 100% oriented to any one customer. We obviously need to try to share our message with as many people as possible. But this does not mean "lowest common denominator." It means *most perceptive* and ultimately, *most inclusive*.

CHAPTER ELEVEN

TOTAL PERSONALIZATION

SPEAKING TO OUR CUSTOMERS

When I talk about "brand voice" I am not just referring to web copy. The actual words you use on site, in a post, or commercial are important of course, a very direct way to convey information, personality. Great tag lines and slogans are wonderful at expressing the mission and value prop of a brand quickly and poetically, yes. But, I'd like to offer that the real communication between you and the customer is happening throughout their experience with your brand, with or without words. In fact the total shopping experience from start to finish - from the day your customer first finds you in a search result, to the last day they use the product they bought from you, is all part of a grand communication. This is a dialogue that goes both ways and which can and should become more honed, intuitive, and relevant over time.

The total ecommerce shopping experience is the medium.

If in earlier eras, the dialogue between brand and customer occurred across print, radio, or TV, the most important developing mass media of this century is clearly the internet and everything on it. This constitutes a very dramatic shift from *presentational,* one-sided content, to what has truly become omni-directionally interactive, *participatory* content. Insert "No Spectators" sign here. But now, twenty years or so into the widespread use of the internet, we are constantly arriving at new, more specialized methods for interacting with one another within it.

Interacting digitally with companies of all sizes has become a central activity of daily life online. People who shop, people who work for ecommerce enterprises, and all of the people who a part of all the systems that support those enterprises are using those interactions to learn from one another, to orchestrate the movement of goods, and to participate in public life. The place where all of these elements come together, the actual ecommerce shopping experience, becomes a kind of communication portal - a Babel fish - which has its own agreed-upon way of "speaking." The concept of "personalizing" that experience is not a marketing hook, or just an easy way to get more conversions - it's about finding ways to *use technology to speak clearly and listen,* to a great many people, each with their own distinct voice.

How do ecommerce experiences "speak" to consumers? Oh this dialogue is everywhere. It's in the priorities set by site navigation tools. The choice of image content to represent product. The overall aesthetic of layout and text. The specific use of language to describe benefits and attributes. The mechanisms provided for searching, for ordering, for drilling deep into details. The varying tones of interaction with different kinds of accounts. The timing, amount, and character of special offers. The pace at which a customer moves through common tasks, like checkout. The degree of follow-through and support before, during, and after an order is placed. The presence of social voices. The sense of integration with other sites, content providers, and businesses. The sense of ease and flow as users travel from page to page. Track record. Access. Updates.

Across all of these elements, the total shopping experience is expressing, *"Here's what's important to us, here's how we suggest you explore our world. Here's who uses our product and why. Here's our reputation, here are our goals. How can we apply all of this to help you with yours?"* That's the conversation taking place across every ecommerce site, which can now rightly be called one of the key *communication* mediums of our time. That feels pretty big. The digital transaction as a form of *speaking*.

So the approach to communicating with the buyer personas you have identified must go beyond copywriting. It must go beyond any individual ecommerce feature. Though the dialogue will include these things, we really want to start thinking about how **every detail adds up to a uniquely relevant conversation with a uniquely interested user**. This is what will make online businesses viable going forward - elevated, personal experiences.

PERSONALIZATION OF THE TOTAL SHOPPING EXPERIENCE

The more any process is adapted to *me*, how *I* like to do things, what *I* am looking for, the easier it will be for me to understand it, engage with it, and have a successful outcome. This not the same as being told what to do, or being analyzed by de-humanizing psychographic profiling. Site personalization is not, at this time, an omniscient a.i. which mind-controls users into increasing order totals. The goal is not to obtrusively spy on our customers, or even to tell them what to buy. We want them to *tell us what they want*. "Here's what to buy" is a roadside billboard you drive past at 60 mph. "Is this what you need?" is the start of a personal and meaningful conversation.

In this way, site personalization is more about a back and forth of questions, answers, and logical next steps.

Recommendation "engines" - algorithms which drive various automated functions in the ecommerce platform - use a set of variables to make suggestions about where a user should go or what they buy next. The most common form of this is a "recommended products" block, which might use the tags you have assigned to products as a guide for which upsells to show users who purchase those products. There is still a very human element to this, as you as the seller will inform your ecommerce platform that there is a connection between sales of lawn mowers and sun hats, to reference our earlier example, or perhaps that someone who purchases after browsing the "best seller" page would probably like to see what else is popular. Software can't make those creative mental leaps - yet. It's your *human* understanding of and intuition about your customers' motives that drives the process, which can then be honed over time based on results. **Ecommerce is more inherently interactive than earlier forms of presentational internet content, such as a blog.** We want people to do more than just read through, we want them to reach their hands in and sculpt a total experience which suits them.

You can build forms of *self-selected shopping experience* right into the UI of your ecommerce site. For example, arriving at the home page of a pet food site, a colorful pop-up asks, "Are you a dog person or a cat person?" sending the user to a category page which matches their response. This response could even send them to a totally separate microsite which is all dog or cat-related products, so they'll never see any products for the other species. That's personalization. I have two dogs, and zero interest in browsing cat condos.

The best way to determine your buyer's persona is to *ask them.*

Tools which encourage customers to enter their own preferences and steer the personalization of their own shopping experience are incredibly effective. By asking specific questions which are directly relevant to why they are looking at your products, you can build a simple but useful portrait of their persona.

If your customer tells you, "I am a person who owns a 2014 Ford F-150 XL 4x4 and I am shopping for OEM parts," you now can employ several strong personalization features to improve the likelihood that they'll get the content which is relevant to them when they visit your site.

First, you could create an availability group for Ford customers, or OEM parts customers, or truck owners. Then, you can steer what kinds of products, product info, and offers are displayed whenever members of this group log in to their account. Next, you would develop specific automated marketing tracks for customers who fall into any of the above groups. You'll save your time and your customer's time by not sending Ford owners product offers for Hondas. Then you might design a product finder interface which is pre-set to discover parts for the customer's particular Ford model, so when they need to find an air filter, they are directed to the SKUs which meet the standards of their vehicle.

One of our Miva clients, Xtreme Diesel Performance, has brilliantly used these types of techniques to great effect. Asking customers to identify the year, make and model, and engine of their vehicle at the outset of the experience ensures that the products they are shown throughout the rest of the site navigation always apply to their exact car. It's quite cool. Compare and contrast with an hour walking the aisles of a local auto parts chain trying to figure out which cylinder head to buy. Then, compare and contrast with a search for "cylinder heads" on Amazon. 20,000+ results with no way to sort by year, make, and model. This is a nightmare for shoppers and one of the reasons that Xtreme Diesel Performance is so successful. XDP does host a store on Amazon, with a small assortment of universal products, which invariably lead consumers to explore more of the XDP brand for the complete collection of products.

The point is to ask for information which makes the shopping experience easier. If you explain at the time of "the ask" that this is your goal, customers will be far more inclined to give you that info, as opposed to an arbitrary request for personal data which doesn't seem to have a purpose ("Why are they asking for my phone number? I have not indicated any desire to talk to a salesman.").

Letting the customer be their *own* salesman is another great way to look at site personalization. **How am I encouraging customers to "sell themselves" on a purchase?** For example, a product builder which prompts the user to gather together various accessories into a custom bundle is more interactive and precise than general category pages for the same products.

Even basic functions of the shopping experience can be personalized to dramatic effect. Different types of customers might prefer/need to shop in different ways, and you can modify every aspect of how they browse, select, and pay for products to suit those preferences. For example, a B2B account shopper might require a faster way of ordering large quantities, such as a "quick order" form which sidesteps the pages and steps a typical retail customer might prefer.

Once a customer creates an account, we can assign it to unique groups which control exactly which products they see and what pricing they are shown. This is another powerful form of personalization which will seem completely intuitive to your customer - their experience will be full of products and prices which are relevant to them. As with any good conversation, there should be a sense of effortless flow - and good etiquette.

PERSONALIZATION "ASKS"

Blunt commands are less effective than an offer of benefits. So, "subscribe to our newsletter" becomes "Would you like to receive updates and offers which will reduce your costs and get VIP exclusive access?"

Relevant chat is welcome, irrelevant chat feels stifling. "Here is an exhaustive list of every mattress we carry" becomes "Are you a side-sleeper or a back sleeper?"

Interaction creates a more effective dialogue than assumption. "This item only ships when bundled with that item" would feel more open if asked as "configure a custom bundle exactly to your specs."

Giving people a chance to talk is more engaging than requiring them to listen.

So, a wall of fashion model pics would feel less personal that sharing a feed of user-tagged Instagram posts showing the same products.

Overall, asking for favors is easier if you explain *what's in it for them.* "Would you give us your honest feedback about our brand and products in exchange for a 10% off coupon?" "Signing up for an account will make your shopping and checkout fast and easy." "Buying this premium site membership also registers you in our monthly sweepstakes."

As we continue to get a good working definition of brand and customer voice, the tone of the voice (i.e. more conversational, more technical, more youthful, etc.) is less important than the larger sense of a *living conversation* between parties. Your customer is not necessarily your friend, or your co-worker. They are, however, the primary driver of your business, and should be spoken to as such. Give them the respect and the candor you would afford anyone you were in a professional conversation with. Be upfront about what you're asking for and why it serves the customer to answer. "Why" is *always* to improve that customer's shopping experience and move them closer to their personal solution.

PROGRESS DOESN'T AUTOMATICALLY LEAD TO CONVENIENCE

Is "most personalized" the same as "most convenient"?

As we reach higher levels of scale with more complexity of operations and bigger yet more specialized audiences, the customer experience also has to grow and evolve at pace. The sophistication of the experience has to increase, and that really means it needs to be *more convenient* for the user who's using it.

Customers, as a general rule, always want the "auto-magical" concept that we've come to expect from modern technology. They want things to work, and they don't want to be burdened. **They care about convenience, they care about price, and they care about speed.** *Many will happily take 2 out of 3.* But the simple idea of a convenient shopping experience has not always kept pace with the explosive progress of the technologies we use to access that experience.

Sometimes the innovations inadvertently make the user experience *worse.* I think sometimes about how 20 years ago, when basic cell phones first went mass market, before smart phones, I could totally dial a phone while driving. I could operate the steering wheel, reach over to tap a speed dial button (whose physical position I already had clear muscle memory of), and I wouldn't even have to look down for a second. In the days when "car phones" were still permanently wired to center consoles, there wasn't much of a national conversation around "distracted driving" because the problem didn't really exist as we know it now.

The smart phone I have in my pocket now is leagues more sophisticated than that original hard-wired car phone. A marvel of usability innovations have placed the sum total of all human knowledge and access to instant communication with nearly all other people on earth into my pocket. And guess what - I cannot easily dial my mom's phone number while driving a car, without risking an accident.

Just the simple act of unlocking my phone, accessing the favorites column, and placing a call hands-free requires several steps and sustained visual contact with the phone. This example isn't really about driving, it's about how complexities bring, well, *complexity* - and when this idea is applied to shopping experiences, we find ourselves in a moment when customer choice is so varied, the technology so precise, that personal interaction with shopping can actually be far more complex and inconvenient than it was in more rudimentary times.

There is a baseline level of distraction now which sucks up an immense amount of our mental resources. Because of that, the modern consumer is increasingly placing a higher value upon convenience. As businesses grow and evolve, offering more items in more ways, this need will only ever increase.

SCALE CAN BRING MORE FRICTION FOR CUSTOMERS

As your business grows, you have to keep asking yourself, at each one of your scaling inflections, *what is the ultimate goal?*

I can think of many highly successful 1 - 3 person ecommerce companies that would be ill-advised to try to go to 10, *because it won't improve the customer experience.* The same goes for some 10-employee companies considering leaping to 50.

If a business is going to make the jump from one tier to the next, they really need to ask, *what is my customer is going to get out of this move?* Are we, as a company, reaching to get more profit, or more market awareness, or more brand awareness? Which of these serve customer satisfaction and which don't?

For a lot of growing companies that are afraid of being copied and devoured by mega-consumer brands, the internal goal is often to simply get as big and well-known, as fast as possible, before the major players can counter-punch. **Due to this hungry, rapid growth, good customer experience may become compromised.**

A good example of a company up against this balancing act would be Dollar Shave Club. Companies like this which are trying to attack the traditional consumer packaged goods market, with the unique modern flair of ecommerce direct-to-consumer marketing, care about having a great customer experience as much as they care about scale. But they really are in a race against the clock. They need to get big enough, fast enough, before they're counter-punched by their major competitors - and customer-centric service features may get short shrift in the process. The risk is if they don't accomplish their growth goal fast enough, they'll have reduced their customer experience pointlessly, be behind their competitors, and their customers will be unsatisfied. Lose-lose all around.

Dollar Shave Club is really outstanding at maintaining a good balance as it gobbles up market share. But we still find that the complicated, sometimes aggressive expansion most businesses attempt is at cross-purposes with a customer's goal, which as we've talked about before, is pretty much always **to get the best solution for their problem, as conveniently as possible.** That goal has nothing to do with whether or not a company is meeting its sales goals for this quarter.

In a perfect, Shangri La world, the answer would be "Oh, if you just serve your customers slavishly, unicorns and rainbows will come forth." I wish that fealty-to-all-things-customer was always the only factor, but that's not always the full truth. Those quarterly sales goals *are* important, and the "everything else" back-end of a business which is invisible to a customer is also important, in that it all does ultimately serve that customer. **But if you make the decision to not put your customers first in any aspect of your business, you are fundamentally risking your business, either in the short or long run.**

If your goal is to just have a defensible business which pays you reasonable margins, what I would call the "traditional lifestyle" business, then I think you're generally going to be more in line with customer satisfaction. I think at that level, your ability to keep your purpose completely, directly correlated to customer satisfaction is probably very high. Conversely, to the extent that you're trying to leverage new technology in a race against time with big companies, I think your ability to stay perfectly aligned with customer satisfaction varies throughout the cycles. In a sense, chasing that purpose, and achieving that balance, is your work.

9 WAYS TO LISTEN

DEVELOP BUYER PERSONAS

Start with one of the key products in your catalog, then apply these criteria to gain insight into who needs it and why.

01 SPECIFIC PROBLEMS
which this product solves, and who traditionally has these problems.

02 REGIONS, SEASONS, CONDITIONS
in which this product is used.

03 SPECIAL KNOWLEDGE
that might be required to use this product.

04 HISTORICAL CUSTOMERS
who have bought this product in the past.

05 AGE OR GENDER
which might naturally use this product.

06 PROFESSIONS OR HOBBIES
of those who traditionally use this product.

07 PERSONAL STYLE
of the person to whom the aesthetics of this product might appeal.

08 ESTABLISHED CHANNELS
through which this product is commonly bought.

09 PRICE POINT
appeal to an economical, quality-driven, or luxury customers.

CHAPTER TWELVE

ETHICAL MARKETING & HUMAN DATA

CUSTOMER-CENTRIC MARKETING

"How often should I email?"

This is a deceptively simple question. On the surface level, we can always point to statistics... *There is a 1 -3% variation in email open rates based upon day of the week. The average click-through percentage hovers in the low 20s. Mobile devices may account for as much as 50% of email opens. 20% of marketing emails go directly to the spam folder of most email clients.* This is all interesting information, and from it, a lot of web content would suggest that you reverse-engineer those numbers to achieve the maximum amount of success with an email marketing campaign. But while it may be possible to manipulate the number of opens or click-thrus with strategic scheduling and souped-up formatting, *this does not constitute successful marketing*. It is a snake oil hack which disregards the entire point of marketing, at the expense of sustainable business models. **Jacking up the stats is not a substitute for delivering the right message in the right way.**

The goal of all marketing is to communicate one simple message: *"I can solve your pain."* Whatever form your marketing takes, whatever platforms you use, however much you spend, let it all *always* come from this place, and be motivated by this message. That's a very different approach from "we have to send three emails per week and Thursday is available." The difference gets to the heart of a new perspective on ecommerce marketing.

Brand intention should align with customer intention.

We can see how well these two line up by looking at a company's marketing efforts. If one side is saying, "I desperately want to sell any of you anything," and the other side is saying "I want to find out if you can help me solve my problem" the essential mismatch will cause a dissonance that ultimately repels the customer. Impersonal wars of attrition on an email list are more likely to end up with spam flaggings than conversions.

So how do you re-orient your outreach to line up with what customers want to hear? Look, you cannot beat the ad budget of Apple. But you can apply a deep understanding of where your customer is coming from in order to create marketing that lands. *This has much more to do with your ethical point of view than your understanding of internet traffic timetables.*

By "ethical," many marketers think we simply mean, "how not to be annoying." What is the absolute upper limit for how persistent I can be before I seem obnoxious? How obnoxious can I get away with being before I seem offensive? And on and on. The problem with these questions is, **they treat the customer like a fool you are trying to "get one over" on**, and this is a toxic foundation for any kind of enduring relationship you might want to have with them.

Ethics in marketing come down to reconciling what the priority of your brand is and who its loyalty is awarded to. Are you an advocate for the customer? Is the customer goal of "solve problems" identical to the brand goal? If so, how can you communicate this unity with the placement, frequency, and tone of marketing materials?

Every buyer and every buyer persona is unique. Every brand community's relationship with that brand is unique. Yes, statistics say that people tend to open their emails first thing in the morning. Yes, traffic to many sites is lower on the weekends. But don't let this kind of hindsight dictate how and when you speak to your customer. Here's a great rule of thumb:

When you have something relevant to say, say it.

This is really the ultimate *ethical* point of view.

Observe the difference between these two approaches to marketing: "Here is what I'm selling" vs. "Here is what you are looking for." While the former ignores (disrespects) the customer, the latter is harmonized with the customer. The former is noise that will be mentally grouped with the endless sales content any internet user encounters everyday. The latter is customer-centric messaging which makes the brand and its products incredibly relevant.

This is a flavor, not the letter of the law. I'm not suggesting that every line of ad copy and every email subject line literally say "here is the deal you've been looking for," because that too is spammy and noisy. I am saying that **an overall marketing approach which originates with customer solution will be more effective than one that is not.**

This is the core of a marketing concept that prioritizes content *relevance* over all else, as a means of harmonizing with the customer.

In "ancient" times, a seller might have designed that roadside billboard ad I suggested above, which stated their product details with as broad appeal as possible. "Call us today for the latest deals om mattresses." This seller would be relying upon a numbers game that *x* number of the motorists who randomly drove past that billboard might need a mattress that day, write down the phone number, and remember to call it when they got home. It's a very "me" approach. *Here is my product, I hope that some of you will like it.*

Conversely, Casper.com can very specifically show their mattresses to Facebook users who have been browsing the mattress pages of department stores in the previous 3 days. Which seller is more likely to get the sale?

Today, we use targeting to narrow down who we show digital marketing content to. Segmenting of audiences based upon data is a good start - but it doesn't get us all the way to true relevance unless the content we are showing to those segments speaks to the *reasons* that specific group is in the market. It is not enough to say, "I sell a lot of products to 20-somethings, so I will target my marketing campaigns to a sifted audience comprised only of 20-somethings."

Why does your product appeal to this group? What are the specific concerns they bring to the table? This is a "you" approach. *What do you need? What would make you happy? How can I empathize with, show respect for, and deliver solutions to you?*

TOTAL TRANSPARENCY

This makes me question if the larger point of marketing is simply to let the customer know that their experience and satisfaction have been prioritized. I think you could really boil the point of marketing down to being, to cause someone to realize that they want my product, yes, but also that my store is the best place to buy it. In other words, "you'll have the best possible experience at my store."

Of course, that gets very nuanced the deeper you dive into it. There are many ways of educating consumers about products, and many ways to express the importance of their satisfaction. To the extent that you're not in integrity with these aims, both of them, customers will feel it, they'll know. There's systemic business risk in trying to convince a customer that their satisfaction is your highest priority when it's not.

Can you take that idea all the way to the end of the argument and say, well then you must be 100 percent transparent at all times and in all communication with the customer? There are certainly people who take that tack. My personal opinion is total transparency is not always beneficial to the customer. Total transparency is sometimes counter to *convenience,* if only because "TMI" is utterly beside the point of the customer's visit. If I buy something at a drugstore and wish the cashier to "have a nice day," I probably don't then need to hear a recap of that afternoon's store staff meeting. I just want to take my purchase and be on my way. So, **transparency must be balanced with relevance, in service of convenience.** That's a terrific guideline.

MARKETING USE AND ABUSE

With this all in mind, our handbook of marketing best practices really hinges on *what aligns with the customer's goals the best.* No matter which venue you speak in, the guiding principle - the ethical approach - views marketing as an ongoing conversation, bound by relevance and respect. In the two most common forms of digital marketing, SEO/SEM and emails, there is a tendency to lose this plot.

Search Engine Optimization is one area of an overall marketing plan which is frequently abused, misused, and ironically, at cross-purposes with the customer's only goal: get relevant information to solve my problem. Yes, the thoughtful use of keywords, linkage, site organization, and meta-data for the purpose of ranking higher in search results than competitors is essential. These concepts were deduced over twenty years of observation and educated guesses, as Google's business model relies upon not revealing the exact criteria it takes to rank. But stuffing keywords into your site copy to match the AdWords campaign you just invested in actually works to *obscure and reduce* the relevance of your content for users.

Having to wade through content which reads like it was written by a machine for a machine is a good way to turn off a human.

Relevant content must *always* supersede trying to out-think the inscrutable Google algorithm. In an ideal world, you want consumers to find you in searches because you are offering what they are looking for, not because you gamed the system. You'll never build an enduring customer relationship that way.

Misuse and abuse are also common with the sending of marketing emails. Even with all of the developing modes of communication available, email marketing is still primary for most brands. It's relatively inexpensive to run these campaigns (after design hours, MailChimp fees, and the years-long investment in building email lists), and as a result there are a lot of less-relevant, over-done email campaigns running. Don't email every time the wind blows. Be short and sweet in your subject lines, and leave the clickbait in the drawer for another day. We never want to harass or trick customers into engaging. But when there is a subject to talk about that's relevant to a given audience, let go of the reigns. Two amazingly relevant and creative emails in one day are better than seven non-relevant emails sent every day of the week.

Ideally, our content should be so creatively relevant that your audience has *no choice* but to click through.

PAID CONTENT

When it comes to paying for marketing content, the raised stakes of a significant financial investment can often lead to increasingly reckless disregard for the customers these campaigns are for. Meaning, **the pressure to increase ROI on ad spend, in the form of conversions, creates a drift away from ethical best practices.** Unsustainable come-one-come-all flash sales, well below margin. Obnoxious frequency. Rushed supporting materials like landing pages and display ads which are not up to the quality standard of high-level brand content. These common pitfalls are enormous drains of marketing budgets, with limited returns.

The difference between "tricking" someone into a click, and trying to get relevant content in front of the right audience, is vast. **Google's relevance scores** were implemented to encourage advertisers *away* from manipulative content. Of course, a new discipline was then born to try to out-game the relevance score, which I find hilarious. But we do not want to let fear of Google drive the content we put out, any more than we want it driven by "get a click at all costs." The balance between the two always comes down to what words and images express the value of this product for this customer. *The more of a bullseye the content is, the higher the scores will be, the more impressions can be bought for cheaper.*

Advertising on social media brings the ability to run professionally constructed high-exposure campaigns which can realistically reach millions of users with an incredible degree of specificity. Is this the same as a *honed* conversation with a specific buyer persona? It can be, but with some serious caveats. While Facebook's Ad Manager is a very sophisticated targeting tool, the service is expensive. Facebook's ad credit lines, frequently awarded in the 100s of thousands of dollars, can be a treacherous quicksand for any business - precisely *because* of how good the targeting is. The allure of being able to deliver a tailored message to everyone in a given age group, gender, or geo, cross-referenced with cultural interests and friend groups, is powerful. These tools were inconceivable just a few years ago, when television was the primary medium for all advertising. But the expense, combined with the dubious relevance of most "likes" (Are people who clicked on Shania Twain's artist profile really more likely to buy skin cream?), again pressures sellers to lean harder on manipulative, broad content, and away from the more idiosyncratic conversations which are possible on social platforms. This money might be better spent by stepping outside of mass media platforms which use retargeting, and looking for niche venues that more directly speak to your exact audience and their needs (such as trade pubs).

WEB OF INFLUENCE

Outside of all that spending, of course most businesses are hoping that organic heat around products will take hold, and make ad buys unnecessary. The press and buzz a brand can get from blogs, reviews, social mentions, endorsements, and influencer features is an outstanding building block for telling the story of products which matter to the world and not just to the brand.

Aside from cold-mailing a hit list of these venues, **the best way to capture the notice of larger organic audiences is by engaging in highly personalized communication with established fan communities.** This can consist of sponsoring events, collaborating with complementary brands, positioning your brand as a subject expert with instructional content on YouTube, blogs, etc., and of course, developing a strong social media presence. If all goes well, this type of outreach can spur fans to do much of the promotion for you, but you most certainly will have to pay for the privilege of getting your brand in front of them in the first place.

I'm pretty sure that the word "influencer" will very rapidly become a joke about the ridiculous marketing tactics of the 2010s. Paying an Insta-celeb $10,000 to hold up your tube of diet toothpaste is already a fairly bizarre convention of our time. Not because audiences don't scroll through Instagram, but because endorsement by someone whose only "authority" is as a professional endorser seems to fly in the face of what we know about the factors which truly influence consumer trends. However, when done right, creating and sponsoring content on social can be a fabulous way to converse with customers and create business.

One of our rising star SMB clients, Missouri Star Quilt Co., has very thoughtfully tackled social media and it has worked like gangbusters. This is a generational family business that had to find a way to translate a hand-made, passed-down tradition into a form that inspired a massive audience of fans.

Learning how to quilt requires mastery of materials and technique - traditionally these skills have been communicated person-to-person. The beloved matriarch of the family brand, Jenny Doan, brought her knowledge and warmth directly to the people in a series of detailed YouTube tutorials. These free-to-watch videos give thorough directions for how to create quilts with the fabrics and tools for sale on the Missouri Star site. These materials are specifically bundled on the ecommerce site to correlate with the YouTube tutorials, dramatically **reducing the hassle and legwork** associated with gathering all the right materials for the craft. With more than 500 videos so far, Jenny and the brand have amassed more than 130 million video views. Wow!

This idea shows how *addressing consumer pain point directly* - in this case, "I want to learn how to make a quilt, but technique is intimidating to learn and the materials could be hard to obtain" - creates a relevant, enduring, profitable dialogue.

CUSTOMERS & THE TOTAL PRESENTATION

In the modern world, every pixel of content that exists online around your brand - *whether you generated it or not* - is part of a total presentation of your brand in the eyes of the customer. All of it. All customers can fiercely advocate for your product, or destroy its reputation. Really, anyone who interacts with your brand can be your brand advocate or brand enemy, *even if they don't buy anything*. This is a major paradigm shift from even a few years ago. Yelp users have written more than 160 million reviews in the past several years. 70% of them are recommendations with 4 stars or above. Now, about 170 million users *per month* consult Yelp for where to spend their money. This doesn't mean you have to buy advertising on Yelp. You don't have to pay Instagram celebrities to post about your products. **But you do need to adapt your perspective to acknowledge the role that customers and non-customers play in establishing your total online presence.**

We might even go so far as to say what you post on your own brand's Facebook page is now less important than what the general public posts. Once you begrudgingly accept that you can no longer control the avalanche of social content which will be created and attached to your brand without your approval, **re-orient to what you *add* to the conversation rather than trying to *control* the conversation.** Again, it all comes down to an awareness of what real people think and need - this being the ultimate driver of marketing.

Your customer is your salesman.
Your customer is your CEO.

In other words, the value of your business is often best communicated by those it benefits. Act decisively upon what the voice of the customer is telling you. And then let them know that you did. A responsive, open-to-listening brand is a brand that's alive and a part of the conversation of the world. A stiff, controlling, and tone deaf brand will *snap* under the weight of its own resistance. And on Amazon, the reality for the vast majority of sellers is that there is no place to speak in the brand voice whatsoever. I find this to be a fundamental flaw in mass marketplaces which will, in time, contribute to their decline.

Customers don't actually care which button gets them to their product, as long as they feel serviced, supported, respected, and listened to. Your marketing sets the stage for this wave of positive emotion before they even get to your site, and assures it will happen once they get there.

Ultimately, you don't really need to worry about your marketing budget until you not only solve for your customer's pain points, but have developed a strong idea of who that customer is, and how/where they like to shop. Then, marketing is like turning up the volume, amplifying what you've already got. *There's no reason to amplify the music before you've written the song*. There's no reason to spend all of your resources promoting the product before you understand who it's for.

Visa and Coca Cola have perfected their products and articulated their audiences over 60 years and 130 years, respectively. With their omnipresent advertising, these brands are now amplifying a product message to a community they have been developing for *generations*. You don't need to wait 60 years to make an ad buy. But your money will go further if your fundamental understanding of your customer is already in place when you do. And oh that's when the fun begins!

HUMAN DATA

A lot of the words our industry uses to discuss ecommerce customers are fairly dehumanizing - "targeting," "converting," "solving," "influencing," "leveraging," etc. The visitors to our online stores are "users." The moving around of customer information is called "resource management." And customer interest is bought and sold in a hypothetical "attention economy." Some of the jargon has come about to describe some pretty complex concepts with metaphor. Other times, we might use this language to imply that the human element of doing business - the shopper - can be *predicted* or *controlled*, as if they were a math equation. But it's important that we never lose sight of what we're really talking about, which is *real people*, individuals who come to our businesses by choice in search of better solutions to their problems. Whether they are retail consumers or are shopping for other businesses doesn't matter - what matters is that we treat our customers, and the information we collect about them, with the respect and sensitivity which must be afforded to human beings.

Every technique we've talked about in this section, from determining buyer personas, to building ecommerce experiences around them, to marketing, all use customer data to inform decisions. This is not a new phenomenon. What's called "customer data" today was just "observation" not that long ago. I remember making long lists of customer attributes on a legal pad after client meetings in the 90s, trying to draw connections between who needed what and how they interacted with the sales process and why. Today's tools for gathering information around customers are shockingly granular, and can be automated to a fault. This is an enormous asset for developing concise and gratifying shopping experiences, one which simultaneously requires a nuanced application and a delicate hand. **It is better to use data to supplement, support, refine, and challenge the ideas you already have about your customer, rather than let the data be the origin of those personas.**

THE PRIVACY DRAGON

Here's the issue. It's the end of the 2010s and we've got a serious problem on our hands. The total saturation of almost all online experiences with personal data has become a profound challenge to well-established ideas about privacy. Much of the current debate centers on private individuals' exposure to hacks, and bad actors who nefariously weaponize the data they steal. Whether these crimes are financial, political, or motivated by revenge (i.e. "doxxing"), the sheer volume of personal information that has been voluntarily offered in the modern era is obviously ripe for misuse. However, there is another facet of this cultural moment that bears looking at.

In the world of ecommerce, we rely upon all sorts of data to, as suggested above, support and develop our ideas about what customers need and how well we're doing at fulfilling that need. There is nothing nefarious about it - the goal is to connect the right content with the right audience, and to empower businesses to thrive through excellence at the endeavor. All of the data collection that occurs within an ecommerce platform, or a tertiary system like a CRM, is intended to make shopping experiences more effective for all parties. Even still, **the line between helpful and invasive can get blurry**, especially for customers.

Almost every website contains some form of sponsored content, whether it is a display ad, a boosted post, or a prioritized search hit. You could say that ecommerce sites as a whole are sponsored, by the sellers which produce them. Given the reality that all internet users will encounter ads every day, it's easy to ask consumers, "would you rather see ads for products that are relevant to you, or ones which have nothing to do with you?" Of course we want all content that passes before our eyes to be as relevant and interesting to us as possible. So in other words, we have a sort-of blessing to use data to produce more relevant ads. The debate gets a little trickier when that content exists to steer people into decisions they may not have made otherwise, and do so by "raiding the piggybank" of a user's personal data. Is it invasive to offer someone a sale on a wristwatch, even though they aren't shopping for one, because they once liked a Facebook post by Philippe Patek?

The difference between "being a helpful component" versus "exploiting holes in the system for gain" comes down to intention. Sending out a sponsored post to your business Facebook page's fans is a reasonable use of the personal information those people have offered. Sending the same post to the friends of those people, on the hunch that "birds of a feather flock together," is less cut and dry, as those people didn't ask to contacted, but they did consent to looking at content which their friends enjoy. Finally, purchasing a "black hat" list of Facebook accounts that had clicked a "Buy Now" call-to-action button on a rival brand's product ad, and then DMing them with a discounted version of the same product, would be a clear violation of both the TOS and the people's core trust in the platform's data protections. These are extremes, but there is a broad spectrum from one end to the other, with most use of personal data lying in the grey. For this reason, it's incumbent upon us as ecommerce professionals **to stay aligned with the use of data which has a direct benefit for the people it "targets."**

The reason for this is two-fold: one, this approach is consistent with ethical business practices. Quite simply, this is *who we want to be*. Two, *it just works better*. Asking for, collecting, analyzing, and repurposing data in an ecommerce or marketing context is far more effective in the long run when it is used to improve shopping experiences, rather than to temporarily pump up reactive behavior without consent.

SUPPLIED CUSTOMER DATA

If the purpose of collecting the data is to make life easier for the customer, it adds value to their solution. So a good question to ponder about asking for customer data is, *will this make my customer's life easier?* That's a simple and very fair criteria. The same goes for any biographical or demographic data a customer might provide, such as indicating their age or income bracket on an account profile. Are you planning to use their age to personalize their experience, by showing them products which you think are a good fit for their group? Will this make it easier for them to find what they are looking for?

If they give you their email address on your newsletter popup, it is fair for them to expect to receive your newsletter. If they tell you they have a toddler, they are letting you know they'd like to see suitable toys. Reviews which customers leave for products also become a form of voluntary data about likes and dislikes. All of these things start to build a portrait - created by the customer - of who they are and what they are interested in. This information can guide product research and development, and help inform sales/marketing strategy. All fair game.

OBSERVED AND PURCHASED CUSTOMER DATA

Then, there is data which is not supplied by the customer, but is instead *observed* by the seller. Here a business might track and record a customer's behavior while they are on a website. This might include which pages/products were browsed, which pathways led to a successful transaction, time spent, compiling of order history into segments and trends (customer hasn't made a purchase in a year, average order value is x amount, etc.).

This is where it starts to get tricky. **In the modern era, all internet users can safely assume that their movement online will in some way be quantified for a variety of reasons.** But while some customers might appreciate the benefits of this kind of tracking - for example they'd actually like to know when a product they have browsed is on sale, most are probably unaware that they are being tracked in this way. This is still ultimately a value add for the customer, if insights drawn from their on-site behavior lead to improved and more relevant shopping experiences.

Are we trying to "quench" a desire they have already announced? Or are we trying to create a new desire within them as they happen to pass through our sites? It's an interesting distinction. The former is the reason they came to our site. The latter, from a consumer's point of view, is a hazard they have to stay guarded against. Which is the better feeling shopping experience?

Once the data collection no longer serves the customer, but *only* serves the company (or the services which profit off of selling the data to the company), we get into much deeper waters. Professional affiliations, response to ad content, and consumer profiles (i.e. car brand or insurance carrier) are all compiled by agencies devoted to market research, and sold back to businesses for use in marketing campaigns. All social media advertising platforms also engage in selling this kind of observed data, in the form of stats such as ad delivery, number of impressions, click-through, conversion rates, and more. Customer data sorted by demographics, interests, friend groups, and *potential* to click/convert are all offered for sale. The point of these data systems, for Facebook et al, is to encourage more ad buys with the promise of ROI. All customer behavior is sorted by metrics and used to justify the ad platform's fees. The problem with this is that the customer's needs are not a part of the equation *at all.* The customer's behavior is starting to feel more like a raw resource used to encourage more list buys by the seller. Not for getting customers what they need. How exactly is that going to be sustainable?

It is not always clear where purchased lists of customer data were gathered from - it's usually a hybrid of publicly available information and data which other companies gathered and then sold to a "data dealer" - probably with the bare minimum of legal consent (i.e. at one point a customer clicked a checkbox which stated, "Okay to send me additional related offers from other businesses.") While technically legal, merchants should beware of purchasing this kind of information. In my experience, it rarely results in profit. Acquiring new customers from large pools of likely candidates is in a sense what marketing is all about. But **those acquisitions are far more valuable when arrived at through an understanding of customer need and preferences, not from a cheat sheet which disregards those things.**

There is an inherent flaw in "black hat" ecommerce data - it is not as effective as information which is freely given.

Data that was gathered with no consent, or hazy, "uninformed" consent is less accurate by nature - it did not come from the customer's goal, problem, or preferences. It is the result of external entities' *interpretation* of those things, which is even further removed. Contacting a customer with sales content when they did not ask for it *feels* invasive, because it is. **By initiating this contact, you are immediately *adding* friction to the customer's experience with your brand** - the stress and irritation of unsolicited contact.

This is a surefire way to terminate this customer relationship for life. While you may pick up a few extra sales from a paid list, the damage to many potential customers' perception of your brand intention upon being violated in this way will be permanent and severe. So if for no other reason than that you'll sell more, always communicate to your customer that your actions are designed to solve their problems and reduce their friction. *Data that is taken is less valuable than data that is given.*

PRICELESS TRUST

Customer respect and trust *only* derive from reliable, repeated execution of good shopping experiences and product experiences. *Did this encounter bring a good solution or didn't it? Were my stated (and unstated) preferences honored? Was this site and product relevant to me? Were my items priced fairly? Did my transaction process smoothly? Was customer service attentive and helpful? Is the popular consensus (across reviews, social, and other external content) that this is a high quality brand and high value solution?*

You can certainly erode this trust quickly with the intrusive, non-solution-oriented use of data. But you can only build it by offering what the customer came to you seeking.

As a culture, we are continuing to evolve the way we define "privacy." Audiences of the future may shift their perspective on data and privacy in ways we can't yet predict. New generations may happily surrender all personal data because it will increasingly be the only shared language of the world. Imagine a consumer who says, "I *want* businesses to posses all of my data, history, and preferences so they already know what I want before I do. This is my ultimate friction-free shopping experience."

If the over-sharers of social media are any indication, this may indeed someday be the case. However, today, **data gathering does not need to be a war of stolen victories.**

The context of the world changes relentlessly - and so all the moving parts which are a part of today will necessarily evolve in new directions. This includes people - how they live, how they use technology, how they shop.

We are not at the mercy of these changes. With every customer interaction, every communication, every handshake, we as ecommerce sellers can choose a holistic approach to business which is wholly informed by our relationships with our customers. From there, we can collectively move in whatever direction we want.

PART V: RESULTS

More traffic. More opens. More clicks. More conversions. Higher conversion rates by device. Higher order values. Higher lifetime values. Larger subscriber lists. Faster resolution of customer service tickets. Fewer chargebacks. More follows. More likes. More form fills. More plays. Better rankings. Higher scores...

Metrics are seductive, aren't they?

There is nothing quite like logging into Google Analytics the day after you run a big sale to find out that you doubled sales volume and had the biggest number of unique page views all year. That UTM URL you built into your blog? It worked... blog-sourced traffic is up by 100%. Oh and how many orders actually used the coupon code? How many purchases were made in Singapore? How many conversions originated from the Facebook ad vs. from organic searches? All this quantification is tantalizing. Is there some secret roadmap embedded in the stats which will explain why people bought, a formula I can repeat again and again? Is there a shortcut to ROI? Is there a justification for our ad buy, proof positive that all of our assumptions were correct?

The more data we have at our fingertips, the more tempting it is to confuse metric results with brand goals. Especially when the things we are actually trying to quantify - customer need and customer satisfaction with our solution to that need - are so difficult to articulate. It would be so much easier if all of the complexities inherent in why people shop, and where, could be boiled down to an analytics number which can then be pointed to in meetings as The Answer. Because before you know it, targets have been set for every conceivable metric, targets which are then used to gauge success and drive decision-making. At lot of ecommerce businesses find themselves in this modality - *a game of competition with one's own numbers.* Often it is forgotten that the original point of those numbers was to represent progress, not *be* progress in and of themselves.

A metric is an *indicator* of movement, but it is not the movement itself. It's the movement we're interested in stoking. The central question here is, *should the ledger be in charge, or the heart?*

While it follows that great shopping experience = happy customers = more sales = higher metrics, *only* focusing on the metrics robs us of the "why." And without the why, we have no way of shaping a solution for a unique client. It is exceedingly difficult to reverse-engineer a great shopping experience from a stat telling you that "mobile conversions are up this week." Most customers don't know what a "conversion" is and are not interested in the tracking of such things on your site. If your focus is solely upon conversions, and theirs is solely upon a solution, a schism is created between the two of you. **What might have been a partnership striving toward the same goal becomes a war of cross-purposes.**

CHAPTER THIRTEEN

METRICS OF SUCCESS

REACTIVE ANALYTICS

Does your ecommerce site exist to make conversions, or does it exist to solve customer problems? This is not just semantics. Your customer is visiting your site to find harmony and help with their "quest." They are not interested in purchasing from you so that your balance sheet scores a win. **It is more helpful to look at metrics as a measure of *alignment*** - how close are your goals and your customers goals? Moving this needle requires balancing statistical analysis with calm in the face of bad (or good) news.

If click-baity subject line A performed better than more straightforward subject line B, should you only use click-bait subject lines, in order to get more opens? If site traffic seems to spike every time you tease a free gift card offer, do you need to load up your site with giveaways? If adding strong calls to action led to higher conversion rates than on pages without them, should you add a CTA to all page copy? If bounce rates are high among traffic coming from iPhones, as opposed to Windows tablets, should you optimize all of your mobile content for those tablets?

This approach is a slippery slope. "Gotcha"-style bait and switch tactics will definitely work one time, but will they work again? While we all fall for "You'll never believe what's inside!" subjects every now and then, this is no way to forge a successful relationship with a customer coming to you for a valuable solution.

Meaningful site traffic is more important than gross site traffic. Meaning, you'd rather have 1000 people who really connect with your brand and message, than 10,000 who are indifferent or found you through a sweepstakes site while looking for freebies.

The psychology of what goes into all of these clicks and conversions is complex. Ultimately, we want to have the strong case we make for product value to be "the closer" on a conversion, not a click-bait headline, deceptive boasts, or mentally-triggering "Act Now" buttons. Building a total experience which offers strong reasons why the consumer should make that click is the aspirational goal, even though it is so common that even the best-intentioned sellers make far-reaching decisions based upon the most recent statistic they read. **Sudden fluctuations in analytics can be quite triggering!** In our lust to increase those results, we often get tangled up in quick-fix solutions when we should be laying the foundation to build something more lasting.

There is a frequently a knee-jerk tendency to go "all or nothing" with Hail Mary plays like keyword stuffing or "Crazy Eddie." However, if we ask *why* customers engage or don't engage with ad content - and all content - we get a much more nuanced portrait of how far our ad dollars are going in the long term.

In short, always pair your study of analytics with "why." This is the antidote to our collective addiction to numbers - *numbers which rarely tell the full story of results.*

DEFINING RESULTS

What is the most important measure of success for a growing business? Well, the specifics of that are going to be absolutely individual for every proprietor. But here's what's universal: **the measure of success is to set a goal and then to achieve that goal.** As simple as that sounds, it holds. If your goal is to net $100,000 a year, and your business is netting it this year and you can reasonably assume that it's going to do that next year, then you can argue very strongly that you've achieved your goal. Obviously. If your goal is to start the next Dollar Shave Club and use direct-to-consumer marketing combined with ecommerce to disrupt a Gillette and get bought by July for a billion dollars.... well that's what they call a "BHAG" - a big hairy audacious goal, a term coined by James Collins and Jerry Porras in their book "Built to Last." This is a bold example, but it shows how different companies ask different things of themselves, and hence whether or not any company is successful is relative. But it's *always* about setting a goal and achieving that goal.

There are many, many ways to measure movement towards the goals you set. Some of it can be tracked as KPIs (Key Performance Indicators), much is reflected in sales data, while some results are expressed in community feedback.

Classic sales goals include number of leads and number of qualified leads, number of conversions, units sold, number of orders, average order value, customer lifetime value, Q4 holiday sales, pre-orders, form fills, and total value per visit.

Growth/scale goals include site visitors, page visitors/time on pages, reach of organic content, organic search ranking, number of SKUs, number of countries, number of employees, and number of subscribers.

Community-oriented goals include social followers, reach, engagement, likes and comments, number of reviews on various platforms, ranking and awards, email opens and click-thrus.

Results can also be measured by things we want to reduce, such as acquisition cost per customer, bounce rate, abandoned carts, returns and chargebacks, average fulfilment time, and customer service response time.

Tracking the various measures of results can easily become a full-time hobby - but this would be like **obsessively reading the local weather reports and never stepping outside to look at the sky.** The real question here is not whether or not to invest in KPI dashboard software. What you really want to know is, have I defined results with the full breadth of *my customer's goals* in mind? Have I balanced the need for year-over-year statistical improvement with a *felt* sense of more aligned solutions? These are the crucial guideposts for a protected business.

Tracking results is incredibly valuable - right until the point where the expense, effort, and wormholes of assembling this data takes up more mindspace than the actual activities you are trying to track.

Then it will become an additional problem for you to solve.

CONVERSION RATES

How closely should we look at conversion rates? Conversions can be direct proof of how well a set of site features is supporting a particular product. The more specifically we define a certain conversion, the more insight it gives us (i.e. "conversion is any add-to-cart" vs. "conversion is add this flashlight to cart using the blue quick order button"). However, conversion is influenced by so many different factors that it can be less meaningful than it seems. Chasing conversions often leads to site design which is oriented to *getting people to click a certain button*, as opposed to site design which is built to *offer powerful solutions through shopping experience.*

When you look at a metric like conversion rates, it's going to vary more by vertical than just by company. So what really matters about conversion rate is comparison to *industry standard*. So let's say you're selling apparel, and the standard conversion rate on apparel for a $100 purchase price is 6 percent of buyers on your site. If you're not matching that, but your cost to get shoppers is the same as everyone else's, you're going to have a hard time competing. So conversion rates very much matter in that they have to be competitive with your industry, your segment, and your cost to get customers. This is a very different approach than panic-designing a checkout page for maximum clicks.

TRAFFIC

Is traffic a good indicator of success? We'd generally rather have a smaller number of the "right" visitors come to our store than a large number of the "wrong" visitors, with right and wrong meaning how likely they are to see your products as the best solution. At the same time, we want to achieve **maximum visibility in order to build brand awareness**, and cast a reasonably wide net to grow sales. The question is, will the necessarily more generalized shopping experience and the additional resources required to support that increased traffic be worth the proportional sales gains?

Really, traffic and conversion rates are two sides of a similar coin, and again, we need to connect it to goal setting.

For a specialty business with a high average purchase price which is already achieving the metric goals of the business, to get more traffic "at any cost" would be antithetical to their goals. They do not need a million visitors per month - they need to hit whatever target they've set for sales.

If you're a specialty rug business making $100,000 a year in profit by selling to private collectors, and you want to double that to $200,000, you have multiple ways to do it. Traffic could be one of those ways, but also just getting five hotel chains to start buying your area rugs could be another one. Traffic is not going to have a lot to do with very targeted marketing in a niche product where you can achieve your goal without getting traffic. But if you're an upstart bathing suit designer whose business primarily is funneled from social media, the best way to scale would probably be through getting more overall traffic to your website. Not at any cost, obviously. Running expensive display ads on a foreign news network or paying for the clicks of a bot farm is probably not going to be helpful. But certainly to the extent that you can grow within standard costs for acquiring high quality traffic, prioritizing page views would be completely justified for this type of seller.

ADDICTION AND BALANCE

I think we all personally run the risk of sliding into a somewhat *addictive* relationship with statistics, metrics, and analytics reports. I certainly feel the heat of it.

As we scale at Miva from 130 employees to say 500, my becoming personally enslaved by KPIs for how to run the business is probably something that I'll have to fight. That's just **the human nature of analytics**.

Up till now, my company has been informed by a decent combination of KPI and customer input. I've historically cultivated a culture with my customers wherein they can email me directly, but if we suddenly had five times as many employees and six times as many customers, some of those communications would necessarily be handled by customer service reps within a division of a large company, and I wouldn't be seeing the full information every day. Thusly it can become very easy to lose the art and nuance of customer feedback, and just fall back to KPIs. If your KPIs are perfect, that's great, but no one has perfect KPIs.

There's a well-worn theme in business which is, *lead with intuition and validate with data*. You know, Steve Jobs was probably not really looking for data to justify his instincts when he developed the iPhone. I think he held a prototype iPhone in his hand, and he just *knew* when it was correct and when it wasn't. Then to some extent, he probably tasked his employees to explore data to validate certain decisions which had already been made with the heart.

ROI

Your return on your investment can feel like the point of 100% of what you do, and without it, your business will shut its doors, and zero customers will benefit from your solutions. This is the reality of taking on a business. But **what counts as a "return on my investment" may not as straightforward as it seems.** In addition to revenue, a company can have many other goals which it is investing resources in pursuit of. This might be a share price, a level of market penetration, the construction of facilities or networks, funding r&d of new products, and more. In some cases, a company may decide that revenue is less important than these other goals at least in the short run (see: Snapchat). So focusing exclusively on financial ROI in a given period is not always the best indicator of success.

Look, it is very tempting to put your foot on the gas when audiences aren't immediately responding. A good question to ask in those moments is not "am I spending enough, am earning enough?", but "how well have a set my goals? And if I'm not meeting them, how can I hone my objectives to better line up with what customers are doing? How can I maximize the investments I've already made in people, software, and systems?"

Sometimes re-scaling company goals appropriately *is* the return you get for your investment.

Metric movement, and the results it represents, is the specific guide you have earned from that investment... if the metric allows you to better understand what your company is capable of this year, it's a good metric, whether it's up or down on any given day.

CHAPTER FOURTEEN

THE FUTURE OF ECOMMERCE

There is no “all things being equal” in ecommerce. The larger contexts which surround our businesses are endlessly shifting - so when we think about mapping our successes, and planning for a healthy business going forward, it cannot be in a vacuum. In the same way that a seller from 2005 could not have predicted or planned for the rise of marketplace shopping, today’s sellers cannot prepare for a *wildly changing and uncertain* future economy. Or can they?

The venues will change, the tools will evolve. Some will feel left behind by technology, while others embrace it. But in the period of explosive growth yet to come, **we must always stay focused on using our resources to innovate something better than what’s come before.** Creativity - in voice, in perspective, in the way we listen, in the way we identify and solve problems - is the ultimate non-commodity. Protecting your business against the dragons first requires a commitment to this creative, open-minded approach, to the idea that our greatest value to customers and the economy is our unique way of doing things. Our unique ability to understand ourselves. Our unique application of personal experience to universal challenges. All of these concepts go toward elevating our innate pragmatism to a place of confident action - then infusing it with *magic.*

UNICORNS REDEFINED

What is a unicorn? Outside of mythology, we hear this term used a lot to describe the kind of person, or business, or dream, we would like to believe exists... some magical collection of qualities which transcend the often compromised conditions of our everyday status quo. In business terms, a "unicorn" is defined slightly less poetically - it has typically referred to startups which have survived very tough growing pains to become companies valued at *over a billion dollars*. It was called a "unicorn" because for the vast majority of startups, this measure was a wholly unattainable myth.

Today, "unicorn" is thrown around more generally, and indicates a tech company (or more precisely, any company which *relies upon tech* to sustain its business model) which seems to magically tick all the boxes of success, **despite *overwhelming* odds of failure.** Really, we tend to think of any modern company which survived the dotcom bubble and went on to become profitable as a "unicorn" - that's how hard it was to endure the period and how few actually did. I'm certainly proud to include our company, Miva, in this definition of unicorn, and it is. But now that the dust has settled from those early challenges, and **the trajectory of ecommerce has been nothing but nonstop growth for two decades**, is a new definition of unicorn emerging? What is the new golden chalice that today's ecommerce businesses are reaching for? Is it still a matter of basic survival against the odds, against Amazon? Or is this "over a billion" figure suddenly more plausible for more companies?

I think we have to look at the idea of success as more aspirational and constantly expanding out in front of us, rather than a fixed monetary plateau, an impressive metric, or just settling for basic survival during tough times.

Our shifting definition of success is moving away from arbitrary benchmarks like that (somewhat ludicrous) billion-dollar mark, and toward more personal, unique goals. If you start an ecommerce business today, you want it to achieve *your* definition of success, to meet the goals *you* set for it, and which in the process provides for your family and the families of those who work with you. You want it to be truly *sustainable.* You want to be able to carve out a niche in a defensible way, vs. Amazon and everyone else. **You want to grow no matter what season the economy is in, no mater what dragons happen to be circling overhead.** *This* is the new unicorn. And it's a state we *can* all achieve.

Especially at the current pace which information is produced and consumed, we tend to get very enamored by quick, fast success stories. In 2006, BusinessWeek magazine ran a cover story with Kevin Rose, the founder of the news aggregator site Digg, with the headline "How This Kid Made 60 Million Dollars in 18 Months." Without saying anything at all about this man's finances or the ultimate fate of the company he created, I do have to ask, what is messaging like this reflecting about/communicating to the budding entrepreneurs of tomorrow? Should a hard-working SMB business feel "less than" because it's pulling in 2 million dollars a year, with every cent of profit being reinvested back into the company? Of course not. Because the measure of success is not about placing on a "Top 100" list.

The reality of the dollar amount on that magazine cover is probably an equation of an external financial evaluation of Digg at that time, divided by however many founders were known to have a stake. The suggestion of the article though, is that Kevin Rose and the Silicon Valley movers & shakers he represented at that time had achieved some grand success which the rest of us will only ever just pine for. And it was an emotionally effective statement. It was emotionally *very* effective, but perhaps not in the inspirational way it was intended - it is not fair or helpful to measure ourselves against the age, fame, or market cap of this "kid." **I think we have to embrace that *real* success is to set ambitious goals, achieve them thoughtfully and strategically, and then sustain those results for time to come.** *That's* the measure. It may not be as sexy as a BusinessWeek cover, but let me tell you something, it's actually far more unique to find a business that meets this simple criteria than it is to find corporations with billion dollar valuations on paper.

CREATIVE LISTENING

At the very beginning of my association with Miva, around 2007, I became highly active in our public user forums. At first, this came down to necessity - we were only a team of five employees at that time, and we all wore many hats. I was thrust into a role of authority and leadership for our customers, and was the best one suited to answer their questions. What I learned quickly was, while customer dialogue is not a perfect feedback loop or the only feedback loop, it is *enormously* helpful to stay in touch with the collective consciousness of your customers. That idea has really deepened for me over time, and while today I could easily field these questions to our customer service team, I feel like my vantage point, and *my ability to address concerns and requests from a place of stewardship*, is of most value here.

Over time, a picture starts to emerge from these interactions, a portrait of the core fears, problems, aspirations, and successes of our industry as a whole. **It is the very concept of success itself which has evolved, on the collective and individual level.** Once I realized this, I knew that my most important role in this success would be to *listen*, and so I did.

What are our customers cumulatively trying to ask, vent, build, destroy? Whether they are just asking for some arcane bit of technical assistance, or voicing some primal fear about existential threats to their stores... is there some collective yearning coming from the people, from the posts, that one hears over and over again? What are the common goals that all of the people we interact with are striving towards, and how can we help (or stop hindering) them in the pursuit of those goals?

To find these answers, you have to keep your ear to the ground.

Back at the inception of these customer and developer forums, user posts tended to assume a large amount of technical knowledge. Even to the point of the community ignoring content which had the air of an amateur, as if to say, *"Hey, if you don't know how HTML and CSS work, what on Earth are you doing here?"*

Now in the world of ecommerce, that attitude really doesn't exist at all. Yes there's someone somewhere who has to know how to do HTML and CSS, but certainly today there would be no mockery if you didn't - it's okay to be an ecommerce business owner without knowing every technical aspect of developing and designing by heart. Neither do you need to have an utterly comprehensive understanding of macro-ecommerce, in order to participate in these defining discussions. One might detect this shift over hundreds or even thousands of posts, a move away from certain preferences regarding highly technical content. I might see this from a bird's eye view, and over time, use it to give relevant input to a product development team about what level of technical expertise is required to operate various features. I might even pitch an all-new product which required almost no technical expertise to run. The *spotting of the trend* - in this case, the increasing "prosumer-ization" of ecommerce - is the *origin of the new idea.*

Over thousands of simple posts asking innocuous questions like "how do I add MailChimp to my site," etc., larger trends emerged, with store owners moving from being "technical experts with an entrepreneurial edge" to being more oriented to "strong business people who hire technical support when they need it." That was something that you could see in the forums. It's like watching storm systems, and it requires some creative thinking to suss out the movements. The same is true for issues around sales and marketing. You'll see people post questions like, "Hey, I want to run this kind of promotion..." and from the ensuing discussing, we all start getting a feel for what the cutting edge is for how stores are attracting and maintaining customers.

These examples are specific to my use of forums, but **there are countless ways to listen with an ear toward developing trends and systemic problems.** Call it "creative listening." Look, not all goals are universal, and not all obstacles to those goals are universal. But the clues to specific trends for each are there.

Overall, the biggest high-level challenge I'm seeing today is definitely that ecommerce people - all of them really - are feeling the squeeze of the big tech oligarchs in many ways. The access points are all controlled, and the toll fees, so to speak, keep getting more painful. The oligarchs (and I use that term only *somewhat* allegorically) are doing it in such a way that's designed to drive their profits up, and if there's margin available in a product, to have it go to them and not to you. What I say to the community is this: **the way to overcome this hurdle is with confi-**

dence and creative thinking.

As the dragons scale up, new industry pain points will be revealed and created.

Collectively, the audiences of the world will demand better solutions.

A new disruptive technology will *always* come along.

It will be unexplored at first.

Then the brave, confident, and creative will be the ones to explore it.

Some lucky people will figure out ways to make money off of it. These will be the new unicorns.

The old dragons will evolve or fall, with unicorns poised to rise and take their place. And thus the total ecosystem will expand and renew.

THE IMAGINATION ECONOMY

We've talked some about the "attention economy" as a driver of our industry, but that idea, while so brilliant for its time, ultimately has some somewhat dodgy connotations today, because it implies a *cynicism* about interacting online. Instead of human beings looking for answers, it posits that human engagement is simply another commodity to be leveraged. I think **a far more expansive views starts with creative thinking as the true driver of growth**.

To be honest, my very analytical brain immediately jumps to what we might call the "business side" of creativity. I love reading about highly creative strategies that successful entrepreneurs have used to separate themselves from the pack, such as choosing which industry to enter based upon an analysis of which segments are lacking clear industry leaders. Isn't that smart? To me, that kind of creativity, applied to specific business decisions, drives ecommerce. In fact, disruptive business creativity is *all* around ecommerce.

Uniquely creative analysis of the same data which everyone else is already looking at is absolutely key to *any* kind of disruption.

Marketing is probably where most companies, especially small start-ups, are able to flex their creativity the most. With 10 people on your team or less, it's very easy to seize on a trending platform or leftfield impulse and run with it. Want to bet your entire marketing budget on a viral video campaign starring the owner's Chihuahua? Go for it and see what happens, because you can.

Amazon, for most products, is going to be *the opposite* of an imaginative approach. Don't get me wrong - Amazon is incredibly creative. Developing a cultural event like Prime Day to essentially rebrand a garage sale of under-selling merchandise is rather genius. But when it comes to the rest of their hundreds of millions of listed products, Amazon's not a creative place at all. Discoverability is challenging. Product descriptions are crowd-sourced for the most part - and without expert-level focus and guidance, it's all ultimately a morass of mediocrity and irrelevance. **If you have a product you're passionate about and you can apply creative thinking to how to release it to the world, Amazon has left the door wide open for competition.**

Pick any product. Amazon is not going to creatively out-think you to get to market, because they don't have to. Fifty percent of product searches start there, so they don't require creativity. Imagination is essentially a great equalizer here in that while you may need some money to execute a campaign, you don't need money to have the creative spark and keep pulling on that thread. **Genius, in other words, is free. No company holds a monopoly on it.**

The funny thing about marketplaces like Amazon is, they have set the rules up to *limit* your creativity! If they find you exploiting your creativity in any particular way that causes them to lose margin or profit, they'll change the rules to limit it. So, you can't have a uniquely personalized brand page. You can't break free of the standardized product content UI. You can't easily offer unique ways of ordering, bundling, or billing. You can't put an attractive brochure in with your shipments. You can't even post a website URL - since Amazon has 50 percent of the product search traffic in the world, one of their key goals is to just make sure that no one's bleeding *one click* of their traffic away from them.

Within this ecosystem, it does take some creative thinking to keep bending these rules a little, such as **incorporating some company**

promotion into a hangtag, for example. But the bottom line is that Amazon is far more mindful about anything that could lead people to not come back to Amazon, then they are about encouraging creativity.

One really gets the feeling when looking at all of this, that there's no one at Amazon who would wake up and think that their job was to enable their independent sellers to use creative thinking to sell more. And yet for sellers, **new and imaginative solutions** are the *only* way to secure a position with consumers that is defensible.

TRENDING TOWARDS UTOPIA

We entered this book with a big problem on our hands - how do we approach the looming presence of a monster. I'm not just talking about Amazon. What I'm really getting at is how to approach *any* monster, with the tools you have at your disposal. As we sail through the current inflection point which is shifting the world's buying & selling methodology, now it's time to focus upon how to apply those tools to build *what comes next*. However, in the day-to-day reality of right now, we are still faced with some very sobering facts:

Google controls the organization of and access to the information of the internet. Facebook has commandeered the dialogue among humans and their cultures. Amazon has captured nearly half of all retail ecommerce sales and rising. Microsoft Windows claims more than 80% of desktop operating systems, and Microsoft joins Apple and Android in a trinity of power over mobile devices and OS.

What will come of these titans in the approaching decades? Will they continue to strengthen and expand market share and interest indefinitely? Or are they too subject to the (economic) laws of the universe? Will they grow to the point when they become so institutionalized that the disruptors and young voices which come in will aggressively take them down? Well, to that I'd say it's hardly likely that Google or anyone else is exempt from the laws of the universe. My prediction is that **in the decades to come, all of those companies will absolutely be disrupted.** They may not go away entirely, but they will certainly morph.

Companies of *all* sizes morph in response to problems.

We see this clearly in our daily interactions with one another and technology, especially when these activities are governed by a handful of megalithic service providers. I used to create my own social network of staying in touch with people, because of my desire to be connected and socialized. It was fully organic, and as such, my methodology was an organically developed patchwork of habits, techniques, software, and systems. And then Facebook came along and disrupted those habits quite a bit. Previous modalities, like group email chains, were no longer sufficient for communicating flexibly with large groups of people, and so a disruptor (Facebook) was essentially called forth from the collective psyche to answer that need. And so my systems for communicating, no matter how rock solid they had seemed previously, changed with the times.

Now, just a few years later, just a few billion registered users later, the public has begun to significantly sour on sharing personal information in this format. Whereas just 5 years ago, Facebook feeds were predominantly filled with observations, emotions, and all sorts of intimate personal information, today we see a shift in favor of less personal material, such as news articles, political debate, and relentless sponsored advertising posts. The problem which this shift reveals is that for a broad variety of factors, the public's impression of Facebook as a safe space to share certain types of content has moved. And so, the focus of the platform has shifted in response. Timeline algorithms have, over time, moved toward a version of the product which favors less personal content. Is the Facebook product the same dragon that it was in 2010? *Definitely not.* From this, we can learn something about the guaranteed evolution of all systems. New problems will *always* demand new answers.

There's probably still some great unmet need in the way I choose to socialize with my online community of people which Facebook is not satisfying. Some new technology I can't yet conceive of will solve for this need in some fantastical and novel way. And in the beginning, I like everyone else will approach this new trend with eagerness and a kind of innocence. **It's in those moments that these previously "untouchable" dragons get disrupted.**

I tend to see the disruption of titans more like *a force of nature* versus something resembling democratic rebellion. It's just the nature of these systems - they become successful because they meet a need. Eventually, via the gravity of their own success, they end up changing the nature of the need. Individual people's needs themselves change. The dragons respond by diverting resources to viciously defend the existing territory that's become so profitable for them. **In the process, they leave a segment open for creative new upstarts to come and change the story again.** So I would guess that the first $10,000,000,000,000 corporation probably doesn't even exist yet, but it might happen in as soon as 20 years.

WE ARE NOT AT THE END, BUT AT THE BEGINNING

All of these changes are already underway, both within the structures of these monopolizing dragons, and by the continuing development of the technologies and techniques which the rest of us use. The speed at which a dragon is unseated can be slow (Sears dominating retail for 70 years until Walmart solves it better), or incredibly fast (Facebook replaces MySpace as the dominant social media platform within about 3 years of launch).

In every case, **the thing that "demotes" the dragon is a better solution to the same problem.** So if MySpace provided a setting for users to socialize with one another, but became too overloaded with spammers, strangers, and distractingly poor design, Facebook solved those problems by refining the exclusivity/privacy of friend networks and standardizing a minimal UI. Of course, we now see Facebook a decade later having strayed from those solutions into a cluttered experience, unravelling over its inability to maintain private data. Now, it shapes its platform to support ad revenue first, customer solutions second. While it may not happen tomorrow or the day after tomorrow, be sure that the table is being set for a challenger to rise and replace Facebook with *a better way of doing it.*

Looking at Amazon, we must realize that when you zoom out, ecommerce has really *just* begun, and **Amazon is just one of the very first solutions that has been offered for customer problems which didn't even exist a few decades ago.** It is the first solution out of *many* that will follow.

The only question for sellers is not how to single-handedly take Amazon down, but to thoughtfully assess where Amazon's game stands to be improved, and then go about improving *that* facet for your own customers in your own way. Ergo, if product discovery and personalization seem to be the key flaws in the dragon's operations, look for ways to improve your site's degree of innovative, personalized product discovery. **Your creative listening to the problems of the giants is a good guideline for where to focus your resources on your scale.**

Let this sink in: you may feel like you've been in the ecommerce trenches for a lifetime, you may feel overwhelmed, or even like you may have come too late and missed the boat. *Nothing could be further from the truth.* **You are in on the ground floor, and the greatest expansion has just barely begun its long and exciting journey *up*.**

The good news is you don't have to come up with a better billion-dollar marketplace. Let that stress go. All you have to figure out is a way to set goals for your own business, informed by the pain points of the customer, the industry, and the rival dragons, and then execute on those modest goals, reliably and sustainably, one year after another. Amazon will not be able to poach your products or customers, *if* they cannot solvc better than you.

We are in a battle for better solutions, not for the market share of platforms.

If your business model is thoughtful and sound, if you choose partners you can trust, if you are honest with your community, and challenge your team to deliver creative, ambitious, and efficient work every day, you have nothing to fear from the titans – you can harmonize with their efforts, take the best that they have to offer, and veer onto an independent path when appropriate. **Amazon has no power to crush your business, or to determine your emotional outlook.** *Only you have control of that.*

WHAT WILL DRIVE ECOMMERCE GROWTH IN THE NEAR FUTURE?

If the last 20 years described the public adopting ecommerce as a viable way to shop, learning to use and trust basic online shopping tools on a mass scale, the next 20 will see those customers expecting solutions which are increasingly integrated with their daily lives, needs, and even thoughts.

Today's "smart" devices and wearables are the very tip of the iceberg of the stunning and swift evolution of connected gear we'll see in our lifetimes. Customers will in a sense be *asking* this technology into existence, for the express purpose of making their lives easier and better.

One of the interesting parts of this is that customer-brand relationships will be strengthened by the expansion of the ways in which they connect with one another, not diluted. The customer won't see the tablet, laptop, watch, speaker, etc. - *they will only see the brand,* in utter continuity no matter where they are.

Personalization of ecommerce shopping experiences, fed by increasingly detailed customer data and supply chain efficiency, will diffuse our current sales channels into a spectrum of unique ways of doing business.

We'll see more businesses finding a way to run *direct-from-manufacturer ecommerce* to a wide range of professional and public customers. We'll also see distributors and retailers developing hybrid audiences which blend traditionally channel-distinct factors like order volume, geo, device, physical retail, brand community, etc. into an infinite number of new micro-experiences.

The ecommerce software itself which we'll use to explore these channels will also evolve. There have been two major trends in ecommerce software - systems which move towards the "entry level" with broad/simplified feature sets, and systems which can handle more complex variables for more elaborate business structures, geared towards customization. The majority of businesses built on simpler one-size-fits-all systems will probably be devoured by Amazon, as they will have less and less reason to exist, as far as providing non-commodified customer solutions goes. To the extent that their ecommerce software can create highly specialized, "dialed in" solutions, the businesses that go the custom route will likely see explosive growth as customers find homogenous marketplace solutions lacking.

This isn't a matter of "which of the strong shall survive?" but more **"who will gain strength by adapting to changing conditions?"** Given the current dynamics, most indies who "fight" Amazon will lose. Those who embrace an economy in which Amazon exists, and springboard off the giant to deliver *better* solutions than it offers, will thrive.

I believe that each one of you has the power to unlock riches, success, happiness, relevance, endurance, hope... all with the power of your imagination. That's what I mean by "The Imagination Economy."

CHAPTER FIFTEEN

LEADERSHIP QUALITIES

"I WANT MORE."

In my career, I've generally tried to foster creative thinking and creative problem solving, just as an overall stance. But then also, there have been very specific eureka moments where an imaginative approach to rare opportunities ended up becoming not just empowering, but life-defining. For me, the most powerful example of this is the story behind my relationship with my company, Miva.

You know, what it essentially boils down to is this: **I felt that I wanted something bigger from life, and I acted upon that desire.** Simple as that.

The details around the purchase of Miva by me and my business partner Russ Carroll is really a story of creative thinking in the face of impossible odds, of trying to find better ways of living, even when the presumed narrative says *"you can't make it."*

I had originally come onto the company as Director of Sales, which in a short time led to the role of VP of Sales and Business Development. This is an incredible trajectory for anyone who joins another business' team - rewarding promotions for being a helpful component of someone else's masterpiece. But it wasn't enough.

I had been reasonably successful in the world of sales, but also had a fear brewing about the uncertainty of my future. In general, sales is pretty fairly regarded as a "young person's business." The stamina and flexibility required to close deals and work around the clock seems to come easily to the young and hungry, with each generation of new recruits more ambitious than the last. This demographic favoring of young people in sales has been steadily becoming more pronounced, not less. Seeing this over time, I really didn't know if the sales route was going to be sustainable for me in the very long term, and I just... *wanted more*. A stake in something bigger. A platform from which to nurture my best skills.

And so I found myself struggling with whether or not to keep this job, even though it was actually paying me well and keeping me busy and on my toes. But I kept hearing this calling from somewhere deep within... *I want something bigger*. I'm quite sure that each and every one of you can relate to that feeling. It's human nature - a wonderful part of human nature. For me, I knew there was more in store for me than just comfortably making my car and house payments, though I wasn't exactly sure what.

Ultimately, the voice couldn't be ignored. On a wave of sentiment like this, I quit working for the company. And while I stewed and plotted and dreamed, I was setting an emotional stage for the boldest move of my career.

This is when I first heard that Miva was for sale.

I'd always wanted to run a business, though I certainly had no rational reason to put my hat in the ring as a potential buyer. A buyer! I was still essentially living paycheck-to-paycheck and didn't have millions on tap in savings. I didn't have a long track record of running successful corporations. I didn't have a roster of investors lined up to back me. But I had experience on the ground, and an unshakable desire to grow.

It would have been like if I had walked into a Lamborghini dealership when I was a broke 16-year-old and said, “Hey, I'm interested in the car.” Looking back, it was all hubris! But there was that voice, imploring me to find a way, a better way, to "solve" the problem of my life. *How can I become more?*

So I decided to try to buy the company.

I joined forces with Russ, who had already been a mentor and trusted friend to me, and together we looked for any creative shot we might take at securing the deal, to solve the "problem" of the sale in a way that might set the foundation for tremendous success. **Creativity was our main currency.** Sometimes it seemed like our only currency! But we persisted. This persistence was the key.

As we waited for the process to unfold, Russ and I would spend hours, days, brainstorming and studying every statistic, balance sheet, and market analysis we could get our hands on. We developed a comprehensive portrait of what we thought the company was worth, in that moment, and also far into the future. We weighed the pros and cons of bringing external investors into the mix, and worked out why it was and wasn't worth trying to get someone else to put money in to help us buy it.

We just kept coming back to, "well, here's the best offer we can make and here's *why* they should choose us." Without going too deep into the weeds of these heady days, it essentially was one creative thinking decision after another, of continuing to pursue opportunity and pull on doors to see what was locked and what was unlocked. We built an offer, and **built a case for why it was the best offer**, why our *unique skills and vision* could take the company to places it had never been. We *solved* for that sale, to the utmost.

It worked.

We successfully bought the company in 2007 on a wave of optimism and excitement, and just enough naiveté to believe that the impossible was possible.

I was looking for my shot, and I had this internal sense that if I did not find and take that shot, I would be forever doomed. And so I convinced myself that I had no choice but to go big. Look, this is a common theme across all of human experience and we see it in every discipline, every art form. I think the lyrics of the Eminem track "Lose Yourself" are probably more inspiring on this point than any business theory paper ever could be... I'm paraphrasing, but essentially he says that you have to take your shot, or you will certainly fail.

I'm really hoping that this kind of moment is going to feel very relatable to anybody who's trying to make a business work, or trying to get their business to the next plateau from where they are. When I'm talking to clients and people who are looking for guidance and advice, there's always a joy in encouraging them to bite off more, to go deeper, go bigger, to listen to the, "I want something bigger," voice. It reminds me of the leaps I've taken in life, the *romance* of **wanting more and going for it.**

There is only one caveat. To tell someone to "go big" who is not prepared for the journey, is to do someone a disservice. But though laying the foundations for that journey can itself be an arduous, nearly impossible task, I can tell you from where I stand now that it is the most rewarding journey ever. **Build something better. Answer something with more clarity. Disrupt the status quo of your own life when you are ready.** If you have the fortitude, it is a fantastic and deeply worthwhile ride.

CONQUERING FEAR

That preparation begins with a simple dream*: I want to get into business, and I want to enjoy the freedom which success in that business will bring*. The difference between "fighting the fight" and "leading the fight" though, comes out of how you tackle the inevitable fears that will rise up within you repeatedly and ferociously at every step of the process. We're human, and the unknown can be terrifying. There is no shame in that. But the decision to either cower or rally in the face of those fears is what elevates some to that aspirational place we all want to attain.

The most common fears facing ecommerce sellers right now are not unjustified and they won't be easy to conquer. But there is a way of looking at our collective concerns as pain points we can solve, with a shift in perspective.

"My products will be undercut/copied by Amazon and knockoff sellers on Amazon."

To this I would continue to argue that there is a direct relationship between non-commodification of products and margin. **Uniquely tailored solutions are far harder to copy - and far easier to protect - than interchangeable cookie cutter answers.**

"The barriers to scale are too high to be practical - I cannot grow my business effectively."

The antidote to increasing friction as you scale is increasing integration. This is the heart of the "complete ecommerce" philosophy. The systems which support your business as volume increases must be linked and centralized with increasing efficiency. Scaling through "times of transition" is a challenge that every business will repeatedly face.

"Amazon "owns" my customers."

The personalized, data-fueled customer experience is the ultimate solution for pain points. Solving for that pain is the customer's master goal, and to the extent that you can offer more efficient and more relevant ways to shop, your customer's loyalty and attention will stay strong and true.

"Distribution-only businesses will be not survive a uni-marketplace culture"

Hybrid sales channels, paired with the dissolution of outdated conventional sales channels, are heralding a new way of sorting out who's a distributor and who's a retailer. Look for unique and perceptive new ways of finding your customer and hearing their voice, mixing and matching from all available options for reaching them.

"The power of my brand will be diminished or even negated altogether by marketplaces."

"Unicorn" success is now measured by goals achieved, not

by market cap. The power of your brand is determined by its position relative to itself, its customer, and its vertical, not by Amazon.

Curiosity, creative listening, and flexibility are true leadership qualities.

THE "FINAL" BREAKTHROUGH NEVER COMES

Throughout this book, I've tried to offer new perspectives which seek to turn status quo thinking on its ear and inspire new ways of looking at the world of ecommerce. Whether you agree or not isn't important. **What does matter is that you stay flexible, and remain open to revising your game plan as conditions change big and small.**

Obviously, there is no single "perfect" solution to everyone's ecommerce plan. There isn't even a perfect solution to an individual business' ecommerce plan, and that's just how we like it. **Our work is never finished - no problem is every permanently solved**. We take what has come before, assess its merits and drawbacks, then create an *improved* way of doing things, until such time as someone can figure out how to do it even better.

We don't always know the answers when we launch a new project. Often, the act of building a store, finding customers, and refining products is how we "find ourselves" as brands and as people. This is the challenge and fun of running a business. **You come out of each experience knowing more than when you went in.**

In a real way, this is what the economy as a whole is doing... finding itself through what it builds and what it can improve.

LEADERSHIP

11 Questions to Inspire Thought Leader Content

WHAT INDUSTRY ARE YOU IN?

WHAT IS YOUR BREADTH OF EXPERIENCE IN THAT INDUSTRY?

WHAT IS A COMMON PROBLEM YOU ENCOUNTER FREQUENTLY WHEN DOING BUSINESS?

HOW HAVE PEOPLE DISCUSSED THE CAUSE OF THIS PROBLEM IN THE PAST?

DOES YOUR PERSONAL EXPERIENCE AFFIRM OR CONTRADICT THESE PAST OPINIONS?

HOW HAVE YOU INCORPORATED THIS PERSPECTIVE INTO THE SELECTION OF PRODUCTS YOU OFFER?

HOW DOES YOUR BRAND MISSION ECHO YOUR POINT OF VIEW?

HOW WOULD YOU LIKE TO SEE THIS PROBLEM SOLVED IN THE FUTURE?

HOW FAR AWAY FROM THAT GOAL DO YOU STAND?

WHAT IS YOUR ADVICE FOR OTHERS WHO ENCOUNTER THIS PROBLEM?

HOW ARE YOUR PRODUCTS A TANGIBLE EXPRESSION OF THAT ADVICE?

CONCLUSION

BULLISH ON THE FUTURE

What we might define as a unicorn today is less grandiose, but far more intrinsically valuable than how we might've talked about it in the past. This does not betray an attitude of "stark, sober realism." Instead, I think it's a gateway to earned optimism.

There are many businesses - which really just means "people" - striving towards this new definition of success. Who will win and who will lose is impossible to predict with absolute certainty. Some will endure and some won't, as we have seen throughout the history of our modern economy. For our industry at large, I'm utterly and powerfully optimistic.

What makes it all exciting for me is this: it's too easy to think we are living in some kind of Orwellian world which is controlled by five companies who run everything. On our darkest days, we might think this isn't a fight worth fighting, because Amazon's just going to own everything in the end. *And that's just simply not true.* It's not true because I know Amazon is subject to the same "laws of nature" that *every* business is.

These systems aren't designed to scale to infinity. The architecture of our society and economy are not built to put Jeff Bezos at the top of the world's largest pyramid. The nature of the universe is such that it's impossible for any one leader to indefinitely maintain the universal perspective which allows them to control the battlefield. Massive scale brings new challenges, and changes the dialogue to the point where previously unaddressed problems are spotlit. It's within those moments that opportunities become obvious. It's in those moments that the opportunities are born.

Really, if you can come to the conclusion that **longevity combined with achieving goals is the true definition of unicorn**, and if you can embrace the independent spirit of "I would rather be in business for myself than for a giant corporation," then you will find these opportunities. Of those who seize these opportunities when they arise, a handful will become the next big companies, and tens of thousands, if not millions, will become the next generation of successful smaller businesses.

So, here we are, at the brink of another seismic inflection point. The dragons of today are hungry.

Your armor: a relentless focus on improving the customer experience.

Your sword: the most sophisticated business technology in history.

Your mission: strive continually to improve, grow, and evolve towards better solutions for your community and industry.

Always ask: how does this ease my customer's pain? How does this reduce friction? From this basis, not only will you be able to justify your margins, but you'll be also contributing to a better, stronger, more useful, and more enjoyable world for everyone who touches your brand. This is the true fuel for our shared optimism, and it burns brighter than any market dominator, or any market.

My sincere hope is that you will take on this mission of imagination with gusto over the days and years to come. Have fun with it! Together, we can build it all.

Join the **DRAGONPROOF** nation!

Visit

www.dragonproofbook.com

for the latest content, strategy, and community resources for your business.

Sign up now for new podcasts, new opinion, new fuel for success - absolutely free and utterly essential.

ad spends, 60, 140
Alibaba, 95
Amazon
  merchant fees, 22
  solutions, 94
  as ecommerce platform, 52
  buyer journeys, 121
  complexity, 45
  creativity within, 170
  halo effect, 108
analytics, 157
  addiction, 162
apparel returns, 32
attention economy, 26
augmented Reality, 52
automation, 49
B2B
  customer experience, 86, 87
  pain points, 87
  vs. B2C, 87
  warehousing, 86
big data, 57
Bose headphones, 9
brand intention, 34, 136
branding
  and margin, 30
  and solutions, 27
  Nike branding, 27
  products, 25
  proving worth, 26
buyer personas, 121
cash, friction, 68
cashless business, 68
channel-specific selling, 81, 83
channels
  customer-created, 83
channels
  dissolving, 81
  hybrid, 88
  open-ended, 85
Citibank logo, 25
clickbait, 140, 158
cloud ecommerce, 74, 76
common fears, 180
complete ecommerce, 39, 41, 43, 47, 55, 74, 117, 181
complexity of roles, 48
content
  and product value, 28
  and solutions, 29
  bad, 30
  benefits vs. attributes, 29
conversion rates, 160
creative listening, 167
creative vs non-creative decisions, 49
cultural adoption of ecommerce, 64
customers
  behavior, 113, 115
  buyer personas, 121
  emotional drivers, 119
  journey, 118
  pain points, 119
  solvable pain points, 120
customization, 53
data
  and emotion, 144
  and shopping experiences, 59
  and trust, 77, 150
  black hat, 146
  creative analysis, 169

data
  observed, 148
  real-time integration, 61
  supplied, 147
DDOS attacks, 76
Digg, 166
digital inventory procurement, 104
digitization of commerce, 64
discounting, perils of, 18
disruption, 26, 39, 169, 173, 179, 180
Dollar Shave Club, 133
dotcom crash, 42, 65
  post-bubble challenge, 43
early ecommerce, 32, 41, 44, 116
eBay, 95
ecommerce industry growth, 116
ecommerce platform, 37, 45, 51
  as translator, 55
  define, 46
  and trust, 66
  retail, 97
  SaaS, 75
ecommerce shopping experience, 125, 131
  communication medium, 126
  convenience, 131
  interactive content, 128
  personalization, 127, 130
ecommerce solution, defined, 47
enterprise, defined, 102
Facebook Ad Manager, 141
Fisherman's Friend, 27
flexibility in leadership, 182
florist.com, 50
friction
  brand, 31
  early ecommerce, 32
  integrations, 62
  marketplace, 94
  payments, 67
  product, 31, 34, 47
  scale, 132
  speed and logistics, 72
  the last mile, 72
  trust, 69, 71
fulfilment, warehouse distribution, 71
goals, 48, 158
Google relevance scores, 140
Google Shopping, 95
gross margins average, 57
hacker safe seals, 70
human data, 144
imagination economy, 169
influencers, 142
integrations, 54, 61, 66
  "off-the-shelf", 62
keyword stuffing, 158
leadership, 177
logos, 27
margin, public perception, 23
margin, strategy, 22
margins, 17
  and Amazon, 21
  and branding, 31
  how to increase, 23
margins
  new definition, 19
  protecting, 22
  subjective value, 19

margins
- unsustainable, 18

marketing
- customer-centric, 136
- ethics, 137
- expressive marketing, 170
- goal of marketing, 135
- marketing abuse, 139
- organic audiences, 141
- paid content, 140
- purchased customer data, 148
- relevance, 137
- social media advertising, 141
- stolen customer data, 149
- user-supplied brand content, 143

marketplaces, 92
master's tools, 44
mega-channel, 89
metrics
- as alignment, 157
- brand goals, 155, 157

minimum viable ecommerce, 42, 47, 52
Missouri Star Quilting, 142
Miva origins, 178
mobile revolution
Monster Cable, 89
net neutrality, 58
non-commodification, 7, 9, 10, 14, 26, 181
omni-channel, 81
optimism, 183
pain points, 14, 30, 47, 59. 70, 115, 122, 144, 180
payments
- "invisible", 66
- mobile, 67
- trust, 65

PayPal, 66, 100
personalization, 128, 130
- a.i. 127

Plant Therapy, 15
price addiction, 18
privacy, 58, 145, 150, 173
products
- as solution, 7
- choosing, 12
- on Amazon, 5
- protecting, 89
- value, 11

ROI, redefined, 162
scaling
- complex retail, 101
- deploying to market, 104
- disruption and scale, 171
- hurdles, 98,99
- inventory, 104
- marketing, 104
- practical issues around scaling, 106
- SMB to mid-market, 100
- viability for SMB and DIY, 99

SCOTTeVEST, 8
Sears, 104, 173
Sears catalog, 6, 24, 28
SEO, benefits and limitations, 139
shipping
- margin, 69
- Prime shipping, 73
- upsell vs incentive, 69

solutions, 5, 9, 11, 12,
- and branding, 27
- and channel, 81
- and commodities, 15
- and content, 29
- and conversions, 160
- and customers, 118, 121, 145
- and imagination, 171
- and integration, 55
- and margin, 19
- and marketplaces, 93
- and technology, 23

Square, 67, 68, 100
strategic technology, 24
subject lines, 157
success in ecommerce, 166
tech oligarchs, 171
technology and product value, 8
times of transition, 102
touch points, 33
traffic, 161

ABOUT THE AUTHOR

With over 20 years of executive-level experience, Rick Wilson has a unique vantage point on the global economic shift to ecommerce, and the digitization of American businesses.

Rick is currently the Chief Executive Officer of Miva, Inc., creator of the pioneering Miva Merchant ecommerce platform. After joining Miva as the Director of North American Sales in 1999, Rick oversaw the company's wild growth to become the most broadly distributed small business ecommerce platform of the time, with nearly 300,000 active licenses. By 2009, Rick and his team of partners had acquired Miva from its parent company and shepherded the business to a modern SaaS platform model, which serves a growing list of enterprise level clients, together generating over $5 billion annually in online sales.

Rick's broad grasp of the complex inner workings of ecommerce, and his keen analysis of the interplay of online marketing, emerging web based technology platforms, and high-level back-end business operations, have qualified him as one of only a handful of such ecommerce experts worldwide.

Based in San Diego, California, Rick spends his free time enjoying the best that the West Coast has to offer, including sailing, live music festivals, and building theme camps at the legendary Burning Man event, which he has attended for nearly two decades. He brings this adventurous, joyful spirit to his life and work.

Made in the USA
Columbia, SC
28 May 2019